Praise for

Jim leads and writes with the heart of Jesus. Humility, kindness, and leadership clarity for Kingdom-expanding purposes jumps off every page of *Leading by Faith*. Jim's chapter on the power of partnership should be read and integrated into the life of every leader in Christ's church, including me! Enjoy this engaging and highly applicable read!

PASTOR TIM AHLMAN, LEADER OF THE UNITE LEADERSHIP COLLECTIVE

Jim delivers what he promises—a personal leadership journey—that skillfully weaves his vibrant faith and remarkable expertise into a stimulating, practical, and invaluable book. There is room for this hands-on leadership book in your library if you are an emerging leader seeking inspiration, a seasoned leader searching for reflection, an inquisitive leader desiring know-how, or a faithful follower craving to encourage the leaders around you. As a friend for nearly three decades, this is the real and vintage Jim Sanft!

REV. DR. BRIAN L. FRIEDRICH, PRESIDENT, CONCORDIA UNIVERSITY, ST. PAUL

Jim does a great job of making a practical application to leadership from the eyes of a veteran leader. He reminds us all, especially leaders, that we "walk by faith, not by sight" (2 Corinthians 5:7), a principle all Christian leaders must remember and implement. Jim keeps our eyes focused on Christ and His will.

REV. DR. JAMISON J. HARDY, PRESIDENT AND BISHOP, ENGLISH DISTRICT, LCMS

Jim Sanft has written the definitive how-to leadership manual for both emerging and experienced leaders within our church, which is all of us. Through the telling of his own leadership story, Sanft adroitly allows the reader to unpack and enhance his or her own leadership journey. Sanft educates on how God has uniquely called and equipped each of us and provides a road map to assist us as we daily strive to serve those He has placed in our path.

DR. KURT SENSKE, AUTHOR, *THE CEO AND THE BOARD: THE ART OF NONPROFIT GOVERNANCE AS A COMPETITIVE ADVANTAGE*

Jim Sanft offers a personal journey of leadership with honest and experienced reflections from his own life. *Leading by Faith* has relatable stories that embody deep leadership insights and is a strong witness to Jim's faith values, which have shaped his leadership style. His journey inspires readers to listen and learn as they navigate their own leadership journey, enriched by their faith. Seasoned with pearls from the Scriptures, *Leading by Faith* is filled with humble wisdom and practical insights from a qualified leader, coach, and mentor. It is a wonderful resource for all Christian leaders.

REV. DR. GREGORY S. WALTON,
PRESIDENT EMERITUS, LCMS FLORIDA-GEORGIA DISTRICT;
VICE PRESIDENT, GRACE PLACE WELLNESS, LUTHERAN CHURCH EXTENSION FUND

Jim Sanft is a key leader of The Lutheran Church—Missouri Synod and a true gift to the church and a credit to his family. He humbly portrays his leadership journey and helps his reader consider new thoughts, challenge old premises, and follow the course God has laid out. Jim beautifully uses Scripture to make his points and leads his reader to think first through the lens of the Gospel and then to the leadership journey. I'm grateful to recommend this book, and I think Jim has done great work. No question his father would be so proud of Jim's work!

REV. DR. TIMOTHY M. KLINKENBERG,
SENIOR PASTOR, ST. JOHN'S LUTHERAN CHURCH, ORANGE, CALIFORNIA

As a Concordia Plan Services board member, I can testify that Jim Sanft is the exemplar of Christian leadership. Each page of his book will validate God's unique plan for his journey, and it will motivate yours. You will be blessed by his testimony and his genuine humility. God owns it all, and we are but stewards, driven by faith to deliver excellent outcomes.

JON BOECHE, PRESIDENT AND OWNER, CHILLWORKS, INC., SEMINOLE, FLORIDA

In *Leading by Faith,* Jim highlights the importance of our faith in our individual leadership journeys, providing great insights and personal experiences that transcend any business environment. It's a wonderful read that will leave you with multiple nuggets to apply to your leadership faith walk.

RICHARD ROBERTSON, RETIRED PRESIDENT AND CEO,
LUTHERAN CHURCH EXTENSION FUND

Leading by Faith is a must-read for Christian leaders! It not only reveals the secret of successful leadership but also illustrates how it can be applied to your own leadership journey. I've had the genuine privilege of witnessing how Jim Sanft has consistently leaned on his faith in God and Jesus over the past twelve years while serving on the Concordia Plan Services board. In this book, Jim succinctly outlines how he has done it while drawing insightful parallels to Scripture.

ROBERT P. LESKO, PARTNER, PIERSON FERDINAND, LLP

LEADING
by FAITH

▪ ▪ ▪ ▪ ▪ ▪ ▪ ▪ ▪ ▪ ▪

Practical Insights
for Christian Leaders

JAMES F. SANFT

CONCORDIA PUBLISHING HOUSE • SAINT LOUIS

Published by Concordia Publishing House
3558 S. Jefferson Ave., St. Louis, MO 63118-3968
1-800-325-3040 • cph.org

1   2   3   4   5   6   7   8   9   10   33   32   31   30   29   28   27   26   25   24

Contents

Dedication

I t is an honor and privilege to dedicate this book to my father, Gerald Sanft. My dad has been an example of a faithful and godly husband, father, grandfather, and great-grandfather. He was at the side of my sainted mother as she battled cancer and is now on a journey with my stepmom as they navigate together the challenges of getting older.

As I write this dedication, he is sitting across the room engaged in his daily devotion—praying aloud Luther's Morning Prayer and reciting Psalm 23. Largely shunning technology, he relies solely on his own version of a GPS—"God's Plan of Salvation"— revealed to us in God's Word!

To really understand my dad, you need to go back to his childhood. Growing up, he was an avid outdoorsman. He loved to hunt, fish, trap, and explore. Although he grew up within the city limits of St. Paul, Minnesota, adventure could be found a short distance from his back door during the 1940s. The wooded bluffs that separated upper and lower tiers of society were directly behind his house. Those bluffs were teeming with wildlife. The wetlands of the Minnesota River valley were not far off. They served as a constant source of adventure for a modern-day Huck Finn. School and, later, work were merely distractions from the wilderness that ever called.

His passion for the outdoors took him to northern Minnesota to work at a resort during the summer. When his chores were completed for the day, he was free to go fishing.

This same passion for the wilderness carried over to his service for our country. He enlisted in the US Air Force and served as a survival instructor in the arctic tundra of Alaska.

He received his own survival training at the former Stead Air Force Base in the Sierra Nevada mountains outside of Reno, Nevada. There he proved his mettle and earned the opportunity to lead and teach others.

In Alaska, he taught Air Force pilots and air crews how to survive off the land with whatever they might have with them as they escaped their damaged aircraft. His students were often pilots, meaning they were officers, and he was not. In the field, however, he was the one in charge, regardless of rank.

Survival training taught my dad to be innovative and resourceful, building upon skills he developed during the adventures of his youth. As a kid, he learned to set traps and configure snares to catch small game. Those trapping skills translated to life-saving measures in the arctic wilderness.

My dad also taught his students to be innovative and resourceful. He showed them that all that was needed to survive was around them. Although they might not see them at first glance, the means to survive were there. It took awareness, creativity, and ingenuity. It took perseverance. Survival in those conditions required mental and physical toughness.

I have never known my dad to focus on what he did not have. We did not know it as kids, but our family didn't have a lot. However, we never lacked anything that was needed. At times, my parents worked multiple jobs—my mom as a nurse and my dad picking up evening and weekend shifts making pizzas at a local restaurant. By the grace of God, we always had enough.

My dad taught those pilots to survive on what the land provided. Likewise, he lived life making the most of what God had given him. And, like the apostle Paul, he learned to be content in his circumstances.

To this day, I do not think that he sees how his example has influenced my leadership journey. Perhaps this dedication will help.

His dogged determination, mental and physical toughness, ingenuity, and creativity all shaped me into the leader I am today. The love and care he showed for his family and friends is a model to me to this day.

My area of expertise is not in the arctic wilderness. Instead, God has called me to serve a large, complex nonprofit that cares for tens of thousands of church workers and their families.

My world is very different from that of my dad. I have always enjoyed being outdoors, and I still do. Some of my most cherished childhood memories involve times in the Northwoods of Minnesota with him. But my calling is not to those woods. The wilderness continues to beckon me, but only as a visitor. My calling and my place are elsewhere.

I thank God that my dad raised me to be the man, husband, father, grandfather, and leader that I am. My hope is that in some way he can see a bit of himself in me and in my leadership journey.

Paul tells us in 2 Corinthians 5:7 that "we walk by faith, not by sight." This is a wonderful description of my dad's journey through life, and it is one of the foundational lessons he gave to me.

Thank you, Dad.

To God alone be the glory.

Introduction

L eadership is a journey. It is not a vacation trip, that is for sure. It is not a quest with some holy grail to be grasped. There is no well-defined destination or end state for your journey. There is nothing you can plug in to Apple Maps or Waze to get real-time, turn-by-turn instructions.

But neither is your leadership journey just wandering in the desert for forty years. The journey has purpose. There are objectives to be achieved along the way. There will be successes, and there will be failures.

In life, and particularly for leaders, the road ahead is not always clear. The apostle Paul provides this encouragement:

> **So we are always of good courage. We know that while we are at home in the body we are away from the Lord, for we walk by faith, not by sight.**
> (2 CORINTHIANS 5:6–7)

And so, we go through life walking by faith, not by sight. As Christian leaders, we likewise lead by faith, not by sight. Do not take from this that I shun strategic planning—or even nonstrategic planning! Rather, I think about these words from Proverbs 16:9: "The heart of a man plans his way, but the LORD establishes his steps."

Coming out of high school, I had great plans for my life. I went to Concordia University Nebraska (then Concordia Teachers College), with the goal of becoming a Lutheran schoolteacher. I had planned my way, but God established my steps.

God's hand in my life is so clear as I look back over the path that my journey has taken. Rarely could I see it at the time as I was walking by faith. But today, it is evident that God was with me and guiding me all along the way.

So it is for you, and so it will be for you. Wherever you may be on your own leadership journey, God is the one establishing your steps.

As Christian leaders, we can go forward with boldness and confidence in ways that nonbelievers simply cannot. As believers, we get to lead by faith! We lead boldly, knowing that God has called us to this time and this place to serve His purpose.

WHEREVER YOU MAY BE ON YOUR OWN LEADERSHIP JOURNEY, GOD IS THE ONE ESTABLISHING YOUR STEPS.

There are many definitions of what a leader is or what leadership is. This book will not attempt to answer those questions.

This book does not provide any sort of formula for leadership. It does not provide a checklist or ten steps for effective leadership.

Perhaps ultimate definitions or foolproof formulas exist, but I seriously doubt it.

Leadership journeys are personal—deeply personal. Your journey is yours alone.

This book is about my journey. It contains stories and insights from my own experiences. I have not walked your path. I cannot give you specific directions or steps to take on your journey, nor can anyone else. You are going to have to figure it out on your own. But don't worry, God is with you as your guide!

Therein may lie the crux of the matter: as a leader, you have to figure things out. You have been called to your position to get things done, to achieve results, and to deliver outcomes. You are the one who is accountable.

So then, why write a book about my leadership journey? And probably more important, why should you read a book about someone else's journey? If leadership journeys are personal and unique, why waste the time?

As we learn from King Solomon, there really is nothing new under the sun. Although our journeys are not identical, there may be similarities. The insights I offer will not be an exact template for action, and what I have discovered on my journey may not be applicable to yours. But I encourage you to take nuggets here and there and put them to use as you build out your framework for leadership.

Adapt and adopt practices as you deem appropriate for your circumstances. Build upon and improve upon my experiences. Be a better leader than I have been!

My goal is twofold: I want to provide an example of what one leadership journey has looked like. And I want to provide encouragement for you on your own leadership journey.

I have been blessed to be associated with many great leaders in my career. Whether they know it or not, they have helped to shape and form me as a leader. They have been encouragers and mentors. They have been gifts sent by God to help me on my leadership journey.

Our church body has incredible men and women serving in official capacities and many more serving in unofficial roles. It has been an honor to serve with and to support all of them in their ministries.

My journey has allowed me to come to know talented business leaders in St. Louis and across the country. I have learned so much about leadership in both for-profit and nonprofit business contexts.

In my role, I get to work closely with my counterparts from other denominations—all gifted leaders who care for the workers and serve the ministries of their church bodies. These men and women are pillars within their respective faith communities. They have taught me much.

I have had opportunities to sit down with US senators and members of the US House of Representatives. I have had dinner with a member of the president's cabinet. I have met with a speaker of the house. I have been in the office of the vice president of the United States (but unfortunately, he had to stand us up due to an emerging crisis). It has been an overwhelming experience to walk the halls on Capitol Hill and to be welcomed by these political leaders. I am humbled to know that they want to hear from me.

Why in the world did God choose me to serve Him and His church in this time and place? The first thing that comes to mind is that God has a sense of humor!

One thing is for sure: if God can use me, then He certainly can and will use you! He knows the plans that He has for you. He has called you to serve and to lead. It is exciting and frightening all at the same time!

Through it all, we know that He promises to never leave us or forsake us.

We can confidently lead by faith!

IF GOD CAN USE ME, THEN
HE CERTAINLY CAN AND WILL USE YOU!

Setting the Record Straight

In 2008, when I started my time as president and CEO of Concordia Plan Services, I had an incredible advantage: I had been the right-hand man, so to speak, for my predecessor. Serving as Chief Operating Officer gave me incredible insight into many aspects of running the organization.

Despite all that I witnessed from that second-in-command seat, however, there were many parts of the job that I failed to fully comprehend.

There were so many things I did not know. And there were many things I thought I knew that turned out to not be so.

Mark Twain is thought to have said, "It ain't what you don't know that gets you into trouble. It's what you know for sure that just ain't so."

I thought I knew what being a CEO was all about. How could I not? I had been as close as possible to that top seat!

But truth be told, I had made that mistake before. There was a time before I was married when I thought I knew what being a husband was all about. And before I had kids, I thought I knew what being a father was all about. Once I got into those roles, however, it was a whole other story!

My dad told me that being a father was the most important job I would ever have and that it would be the one I was least prepared to take on. How right he was!

But as Twain quipped, it is not what we don't know that gets us into trouble. Those things we "know" for certain that simply are not true—those are the things that can get us into tough situations.

There are a lot of perceptions about CEOs, presidents, and other leaders. There are perceptions about pastors. There are perceptions about principals. There are perceptions about boards and board chairs.

Until you serve in one of those roles and take on the responsibilities and accountability that come with it, you really have no idea what all that role entails.

For leaders, emerging leaders, and those who aspire to be leaders, it is important to recognize that many of our perceptions may not be true at all.

In part 1 of this book, I want to tackle some common misperceptions about leaders, the role of leaders, and the nature of leadership.

Now, this list in no way represents all the things I failed to fully understand or misunderstood going into my tenure as CEO. When I think about all I have learned along the way, or perhaps when I think of all that I did not know when I started out as CEO, it is remarkable that the board determined that I was the best candidate to fill the position.

As leaders, we must recognize that there are many things we do not know. And we must have the humility to accept the fact that some things we think are true are, in fact, *not* true. Twain warned of the dangers that come when pride and rigidity chain us to untrue things.

As we move forward through the rest of this book, I want to make sure there is clarity over an important yet often overlooked aspect of leadership: leadership journeys are personal. You come into your role with your unique skills and experiences. Your journey will not be the same as mine. The learnings in the chapters that follow may or may not apply, but I pray that in each one you find some insight that challenges and expands your thinking and understanding of your own journey.

CHAPTER 1

The WINDSHIELD FALLACY

. . . .

I f you are reading a book on leadership, I would guess that you are on LinkedIn. I am on the platform and check it frequently to see what people have posted. My time there is passive rather than active, meaning that I am not a contributor or commenter. Perhaps one day I will develop that routine. But I do like to go out and see what gets posted and reposted.

You can find some really useful information out there, whether from someone's original content or reposts of published articles. There is also some questionable material out there. Certainly not to the extent of what might be on Facebook, but some less than reputable or reliable information does make its way onto the LinkedIn platform.

It is fairly simple to post and to read material, but it is not always easy to discern its quality, accuracy, or depth. Unless you are an expert in a particular area, you might just accept what is presented as fact. Outlandish material is pretty easy to spot. What is dangerous, however, is the material that seems reasonable, or perhaps close to being true, especially when it fits your personal narrative.

Another danger is material that is true in a sense but leaves out the whole truth or fails to contain only the truth. Many political careers have been built on such messaging.

Leadership quotes often appear on LinkedIn. Most of these quotations come from well-known and established leaders, and some come from people I have never heard of (which does not mean they are not famous or experts). Some quotes stand on their own, whereas others are clearly taken out of context.

As with all information on social media, leadership quotes need to be thoughtfully considered before they are applied. Something may sound good on the surface but become a bit more challenging when we think through all its ramifications.

Social media, not to mention modern news cycles, thrive on the short attention spans that plague so much of our society. Sound bites rule the day. Opinions can be swayed quickly by a pithy statement that seems true at first glance. Such statements are read and accepted as truth, and the reader hurries on to the next story.

The Fallacy

There is a quote that has been widely attributed to the late general and secretary of state Colin Powell that takes on different forms but in essence states, "Always focus on the front windshield and not the rearview mirror."[1] Although seemingly inspirational and motivating, it is wrong. And not just a little wrong. For leaders, it is completely and dangerously wrong. And for Christian leaders especially, it is even more dangerous because it could lead us to think we are in the place of God.

Now, I am pretty sure no expert or book-writing consultant would advise a first-time author to challenge the wisdom of a great national hero. Especially one who was a highly decorated general and well-respected foreign diplomat. But here we go.

On the surface, it seems hard to argue with the statement. Leaders, like drivers, must always be looking and thinking ahead. Leaders help envision a future state for the organization or the group that they lead. They paint a picture of the future that is motivating, exciting, and engaging. All of that is true. So why am I so down on the quote?

. . . .

1 See, for example, Jessica Sager, "50 Colin Powell Quotes to Remember the Soldier, Leader and Man America Lost," *Parade*, October 18, 2021, https://parade .com/1280254/jessicasager/colin-powell-quotes/.

Let me clarify that I am not telling leaders to focus on the rearview mirror instead. That would be equally foolish and dangerous. There is a proper time and place for the rearview mirror, which I will get into later, but it can never be the area of focus for a leader.

With all due respect to the late general and secretary of state, the idea that a leader must always focus on the front windshield may be inspiring, but it is misguided at best and potentially destructive at worst.

When we break down the implications of this quote, aspiring leaders might be led to believe that if they always focus on the front windshield they will, like a person driving a car, have clarity regarding what lies ahead. With that clarity, then, the leader can expertly guide the organization safely down the road to its final destination.

BUT HUMANS CAN NEVER KNOW THE FUTURE. AND THEREIN LIES THE FALLACY OF THIS QUOTE AND THE DANGER FOR LEADERS.

But humans can never know the future. And therein lies the fallacy of this quote and the danger for leaders.

The future is completely unknowable unless revealed to us by our all-knowing and all-powerful God! What I know and am certain of regarding the future is only what God has revealed to us through Scripture. I know that my Redeemer lives and that He will return again in glory. With respect to things on this side of eternity, the future is unknown.

Of course, a leader needs to be future focused and forward thinking. This is an essential responsibility of leadership. But to suggest that the leader can see and understand what lies ahead—like the driver of a car—and thus successfully guide an organization or team to some envisioned end state brings great risk not only to the leader but also to those they lead.

Role Confusion

If I start to believe that as a leader I can see and fully understand what is out ahead of me, I have put myself in the place of the One who *does* know and see what lies ahead. When I put myself into the driver's seat, thinking that I can lead with full clarity and conviction, I put myself in the role of God. I risk building my own tower of Babel.

As a leader, I am a steward or a manager of what is entrusted to my care. I am not the Master.

> AS A LEADER, I AM A STEWARD OR A MANAGER OF WHAT IS ENTRUSTED TO MY CARE. I AM NOT THE MASTER.

The steward still must make decisions and take prudent action in pursuit of desired outcomes. The steward is called and empowered by the will and pleasure of the Master and is bound by His constraints.

As Christian leaders, we lead by faith, not by sight. I cannot see what is coming ahead, but I trust in the One who fully knows and sees, the One who has called me to lead in this time and place.

With that said, I am not suggesting that leaders should not be thinking and planning ahead. That is an essential part of our responsibilities as leaders. We are still called to make plans. We are to consider risks and potential scenarios.

As we make our plans, we must also think about contingencies. We attempt to anticipate how, where, and when our plans may not succeed. We think ahead to how we may need to adjust the plan as the conditions warrant. We are nimble and flexible. We remain confident and resolute, yet humble and adaptable. We never stop observing and learning. We apply the learning and adjust as the situation demands. But it is irresponsible to believe that we can know for certain what is coming.

The illusion of certainty also breeds overconfidence and arrogance. There is a spiritual danger as the relationship between us and our God and Creator is reversed. There is also real danger to the organization and the people we have been called to lead.

Sound extreme? A couple of examples come to mind. No doubt you can come up with your own. General George Custer, for example, was absolutely certain that he had the full and accurate view out the front of his windshield. Likewise, the captain of the Titanic was certain of what he saw and knew to be true as he captained a ship that supposedly not even God Himself could sink.

Maybe your decisions are not a matter of life and death like the examples above, but such overconfidence can still cause devastation for others. Companies fail. Jobs are eliminated. Investments are lost. Careers of others are ruined. Relationships are severed. The list goes on.

When leaders put themselves in the place of God and believe they can see and fully understand the future, the damage goes well beyond the leader.

Where We Should Look

Enough law for the moment. Let's come at this from a point of grace: there is no windshield for us to look out that will provide a perfect (or even sufficient) picture of what is coming. What lies ahead of us is known only by God. And we take comfort in the fact that what lies ahead is fully known by our Creator and Redeemer! Therefore, we lead by faith, not by sight.

AS CHRISTIAN LEADERS, WE GO FORWARD WITH FAITH AND CONFIDENCE.

Imperfect and incomplete knowledge of the future does not prevent us from moving forward. As Christian leaders, we go forward with faith and confidence. Consider how God's words to Joshua provide encouragement to us today:

> **After the death of Moses the servant of the LORD, the LORD said to Joshua the son of Nun, Moses' assistant, "Moses my servant is dead. Now therefore arise, go**

over this Jordan, you and all this people, into the land that I am giving to them, to the people of Israel. . . . Just as I was with Moses, so I will be with you. I will not leave you or forsake you. Be strong and courageous, for you shall cause this people to inherit the land that I swore to their fathers to give them. Only be strong and very courageous, being careful to do according to all the law that Moses my servant commanded you. . . . Have I not commanded you? Be strong and courageous. Do not be frightened, and do not be dismayed, for the LORD your God is with you wherever you go." (JOSHUA 1:1–2, 5–7, 9)

Let's put this into context. Joshua was part of the advance team that went into the Promised Land to provide intelligence on what the people of Israel would encounter. The reports came back that the land was plentiful but the current occupants were formidable.

Joshua witnessed those challenges firsthand, yet implored Moses and the people to move quickly and take the land. He knew that if God was with them they would ultimately prevail.

Joshua, as an emerging leader, wanted to move forward in faith!

Decades later, God spoke the words above to the new chosen leader of His people. I take great comfort and encouragement in them today, and it is God's encouragement to you as well: Be strong. Be courageous. The Lord your God is with you wherever you go!

The Side Windows

Having considered the windshield part of this quote, let's address some other significant problems. To suggest that the leader look out only the front windshield negates the valuable information to be seen through the side windows and the rearview mirror.

As young drivers, we were taught to primarily focus on the front window. But we were also encouraged to periodically look out the side windows and check our rearview mirrors. The advice was to glance at them every few minutes and then return our attention to what was ahead. We were cautioned about the risks of not looking at those other perspectives.

Leaders do need to prioritize thinking and looking ahead; that should occupy the majority of our attention.

However, we also need to take more than a cursory glance out of our side windows and in our rearview mirror. As established, we cannot see what lies ahead. But we can learn much from what is going on around us—the side windows. And we can learn much from our history—the rearview mirror.

Let's consider first the view out of the side windows. The side windows give you the perspective of where you are right now. They provide the best sense of the environment in which you find yourself. This information is valuable and timely.

This view could be considered a current-state assessment. Effective leaders need to take a long and hard look at their current situation and then make an honest evaluation of the current environment.

As discussed above, leaders need to be thinking and planning ahead. We have our organizational missions, and we create strategic plans with objectives and long-term goals. But how can you begin a journey without clearly knowing your current position?

Many consultants will take organizational leaders through a SWOT analysis during the early phases of a strategic planning process. The components of such an assessment are simple:

STRENGTHS: Those things you do well or unique capabilities or resources

WEAKNESSES: Areas for improvement or where resources are lacking

OPPORTUNITIES: Trends that can be taken advantage of

THREATS: Looming risks or emerging competitors

Assessing opportunities and threats is part of the forward thinking that leaders must do—looking out the windshield. It involves a future-state assessment. But evaluating strengths and weaknesses is part of the critical current-state assessment. It involves an honest and transparent evaluation of your organization's current situation.

Another tool that is often used is an environmental scan. In this exercise, leaders consider macro factors that may impact the long-term viability of their organization. Such factors may include technology, legal and regulatory concerns, and economic and sociological trends—in other words, realities that affect your current situation.

The point here is not to provide a primer on strategic planning. Rather, I want to demonstrate that proper strategic planning requires an honest evaluation of the situation leaders and organizations find themselves in. Therefore, leaders cannot look only out the front windshield but must also look long and hard out of the side windows.

The Rearview Mirror

Finally, let's turn our attention to the rearview mirror. In our analogy, the rearview mirror shows us our past. As leaders, we cannot live in the past—that is certain. However, leaders must learn from the past—this is also certain.

We must honestly assess the choices we made, the turns we took, and how those decisions led us to where we are.

One of the best examples of this comes out of athletics. We hear about this type of analysis in football, but it happens in virtually all sports. It used to be reserved for professional and college-level teams but has slowly made its way down through the ranks.

That practice is the review of game film. Coaches and teams will review game film, often in painful detail. The previous night's game is broken down play by play. It becomes readily apparent to everyone watching which plays were pulled off with excellence and which plays were lacking execution. Every decision is reevaluated with the advantage of hindsight. The film clearly illustrates the decisions that should have been made.

Are coaches trying to re-play yesterday's game? Of course not! But yesterday's successes and failures need to be recognized so that the team can be better prepared for the next opponent.

Honest evaluation of performance enables the team and individual players to grow and develop. Players see how to adjust their decision making and performance in order to improve.

LEADERS NEED TO SHARE HONEST REFLECTIONS ON PAST PERFORMANCE.

As a leader, you have the same responsibility to your organization and to your team. Leaders need to share honest reflections on past performances. Top players want to improve!

By the way, it is not just players who learn from the past. Coaches learn as well. By reviewing past games, they may realize that they did not prepare their team properly or perhaps they called the wrong play.

Players and coaches all benefit from honest assessment of the past. And that assessment means looking at the rearview mirror.

Called to Be Faithful

One final but important blind spot of the windshield fallacy: it prevents humility.

Humility is perhaps the most important attribute of effective leaders. When done with honesty and integrity, paying attention to the view out the side windows (current-state assessment) and in the rearview mirror (performance evaluation) will help leaders remain humble.

Lutheran Christians learn that one of the roles the Law plays in our lives is that of a mirror. The Law shows us our sin and our need for our Savior.

Honest evaluation of our past shows us our failings as leaders—past and present.

You may be a great leader. You might be the Tom Brady of your team. But even Tom made mistakes on the field. And even Tom Brady, arguably the greatest quarterback of all time, went back in painstaking detail over every play from every game in order to improve as a player.

As a leader, I have been far from perfect. But I work to learn from my mistakes—not just to make me better but also so that my team and my organization can win!

> GOD DOES NOT CALL US TO BE PERFECT. BUT HE DOES CALL US TO BE FAITHFUL.

God does not call us to be perfect. But He does call us to be faithful. It is my continual prayer that I be the faithful leader He has called me to be.

But here also is a tremendous amount of comfort.

The windshield fallacy leads me to believe that everything is on me. If I only ever look out the front windshield, then it is up to me to provide wisdom and direction to all who are under my charge.

Leading by faith, not by sight, means that it does not depend on me. I am merely a steward. God is the Master, and He is my guide!

CHAPTER 2

THERE *Is* NO PLAYBOOK

. . . .

I ndiana Jones is more of a loner than a leader. Although other characters affect critical plot points, the Indiana Jones movies are really all about the adventures of Indy.

That said, there is an important leadership lesson found in one of the many action scenes in the Indiana Jones movie *Raiders of the Lost Ark*. I am sure the line was inserted for its comedic effect. But it contains a profound reality for leaders.

At one point in the movie, Indy needs to rescue Marion from her Nazi captors. The question from Indy's companion was a simple one: What's the plan? The response from Indy was far from inspirational for his friend, whose life was also on the line. But the answer was open, transparent, and brutally honest. It provided important clarity in that moment.

Indy simply replied that he did not know. He went on to say that he was making it up as he went along.

Now, I am not suggesting that leaders do not need a plan. But as various military leaders have said, no plan survives first contact with the enemy. Once the fighting begins, leaders often have to make things up as they go.

I remember making a similar statement once to a member of my team. I do not remember the context or the larger topic at hand. We were standing in my office, and whatever the issue was, the team member was looking to me for some sort of profound or wise answer. I had none.

At that moment, a wave of clarity came over me. Perhaps I had recently watched *Raiders of the Lost Ark*. For some reason, I flatly stated: "You do realize, don't you, that I am making all of this up as I go along?"

The team member was a bit stunned. To be honest, I was also a bit stunned that I had so bluntly articulated the dilemma I faced. After all, the leader is supposed to have all the answers. Leaders are to be the dispensers of all wisdom. As CEO, I was to have the perfectly contemplated and clear course of action.

But at that moment I had nothing.

Although I often quote movies, I was not channeling Indiana Jones. Instead, it was a moment of personal and professional clarity, an authentic "aha" moment, speaking more to myself than to my team member.

Since then, I have repeated that line more than a few times. It can bring levity to a situation or at least provide a moment to stop, catch a breath, and reflect.

A Reality in Life

"Making it up as I go along" is not an excuse. It is a statement of reality for us all.

Plans do not survive first contact with the enemy. Once the fighting begins, a general controls, at best, 50 percent of what is happening. The enemy is also planning, plotting, and acting. Throw in outside factors, and the amount of control drops well below 50 percent.

But isn't this true in all of life? As we take on new roles and responsibilities, don't we find ourselves making decisions that we have never had to make before?

When I became a husband, I had no idea how to be a husband. I have been making it up as I go along for nearly forty years. At our wedding, my wife and I made vows before God to be faithful to each other, and we have been. We did not, however, commit to a specific action plan. Life happened. Plans changed. Vows remain. And God blesses.

Through the generations, there have been countless husbands. There are many books and other resources on how to be a husband or a better husband. I am blessed to have a father who modeled how to be a godly husband. But I had to learn on my own how to be a husband to my wife. By the grace of God and with the love, support, and patience of my wife, I have been figuring it out as I go along.

When I became a father, I was making it up as I went along. As with my vocation as husband, I was motivated by love and had my own example and role model of a godly father. Books and other resources may have been helpful, but I had to figure out how to be a father to my sons.

Fortunately for my sons, my wife is a better mother than I am a father. She is also a better grandmother than I am a grandfather. And God continues to bless!

IN SO MANY OF THE ROLES WE PLAY, THE VOCATIONS WE ARE CALLED TO, WE DO MAKE IT UP AS WE GO ALONG.

In so many of the roles we play, the vocations we are called to, we do make it up as we go along.

There is no playbook for life. And as a subset of life, there is no playbook for being a leader.

Solving Problems

As leaders, we are accountable for three things:

1. **Figuring things out**

2. **Making decisions**

3. **Executing with excellence**

Concordia Plan Services (CPS), where I serve as president and CEO, manages the qualified employee benefit plans of The Lutheran Church—Missouri Synod. The employee benefit world is complex. Each benefit type presents its own set of challenges.

So, the LCMS appoints a board of experts to manage those complexities: the Concordia Plan Services board of directors.

The CPS board meets quarterly. But challenges occur regularly, and those problems need to be solved regularly. The CPS board hires a CEO to assist them in their duties, particularly in these day-to-day affairs. Decisions (within board-approved parameters) need to be made continually. And excellent execution must occur daily. As leader, I am accountable to the board for all of these. And all three are hard.

"Figuring things out" is really problem solving. Perhaps things are different now, but throughout my academic career, there was little emphasis on actual problem solving. That may seem a bit odd, given that my academic background is in mathematics!

In high school, I took the accelerated math track, which included calculus during my senior year. Although my bachelor's degree is in education, I also had the equivalent of a major in math and took every mathematics or statistics class at Concordia University, Nebraska that would count toward my degree. I have a master of science in mathematics and statistics. I taught mathematics at the high school level and at what is now a Big Ten university. But through it all, I never solved one original problem. All I or my students ever did was recreate solutions to problems that had already been solved by someone else.

The academic system I came through rewarded us for finding the right answer. The best students were the ones who determined the correct answers quickly and found the most of them. Every problem had a single right answer, and I was able to find that right answer very quickly.

The system elevated answer finding over problem solving.

> THE SYSTEM ELEVATED ANSWER FINDING OVER PROBLEM SOLVING.

As a result, many people who were good at math in school struggle with problem solving in the real world. They built their confidence by reproducing correct answers, so solving actual problems in the real world can be daunting.

Optimal Solutions

In the real world of problem solving, we look to identify optimal solutions because perfect solutions are essentially nonexistent. Optimal solutions consider what is known while recognizing that much is unknown. Optimal solutions consider the reality of system constraints. Optimal solutions require weighing multiple factors and ultimately rely on the decision-maker's judgment.

Here is a tough but important reality: optimal solutions are based on what is actually known or can be made known.

Many analytic types get caught up in analysis paralysis, overwhelmed by the data or concerned about a lack of data. Perhaps they fear making a mistake. The third servant in the parable of the talents comes to mind (Matthew 25:14–30). Whatever the cause, the individual is frozen, and fear takes over.

Problem solving in the real world is not a perfect process. We can't analyze our way to the perfect solution—if one even exists. Perhaps twenty years later, we might be able to go back and decide with certainty what should have been done, but life does not work that way.

In other words, leaders have no playbook. We must figure things out. We are to use our God-given abilities and apply wisdom, discernment, curiosity, and suspicion to make the best decision.

THE LEADER ALONE IS ACCOUNTABLE FOR CLEARING OUT THE NOISE AND PROVIDING CLARITY OF DIRECTION.

At the end of the problem-solving process, the leader must come to decision. The leader alone is accountable for clearing out the noise and providing clarity of direction. For a CEO, the decision may come in the form of a recommendation to the board to act on, but that is a decision nonetheless.

Leaders recognize that the buck stops with us. Although my board may make the actual final decision, they are doing so based upon my recommendation. Therefore, I must be confident in the problem-solving process. All obtainable information is brought forward, all points of view are considered, consequences are weighed, and a decision is made.

Unique Solutions

I believe deeply that your leadership journey is yours alone, as mine belongs to me alone. We have been called by God to be leaders in our respective roles at this time in these particular sets of circumstances to address these particular challenges.

Unique situations and challenges call for unique solutions.

Unique, however, does not mean that there are not similarities to what others have faced. Unique does not mean that we cannot learn from the lessons of others. As leaders, we want to take advantage of any opportunity to learn from one another's journeys. Do not reinvent the wheel!

It is said that imitation is the highest form of flattery. Imitation and adaptation could be the highest form of genius.

While I hold firm to my assertion that leadership journeys are unique and personal, I also believe what the writer of Ecclesiastes observed:

> **What has been will be again, what has been done will be done again; there is nothing new under the sun.** (ECCLESIASTES 1:9)

God has uniquely created and gifted each of us. We live and work with other uniquely created and gifted people of God. We lead unique organizations with unique challenges. Yet, there is nothing new under the sun. No one has walked down your path, but others have traveled similar roads. Have the wisdom and the humility to learn from them!

> UNIQUE SITUATIONS AND CHALLENGES CALL FOR UNIQUE SOLUTIONS.

Leaders, do not waste time solving problems that have already been solved—or at least have been largely solved.

Although no one has faced exactly what you face, others have certainly met similar situations. Look to how they solved their challenges. Consider what worked well and what didn't. Learn from their mistakes.

Find those best ideas, and then adjust and adapt them to your situation.

To put a bit of a different spin on mathematics education, I will go back to the most influential professor from whom I was blessed to learn. This professor would tell us that mathematicians were lazy. His point was that mathematicians looked to build on the work that had been done previously by others. They do not recreate what someone else has done; rather, they learn from and extend what others have already discovered.

As leaders, we must constantly be learning from others. We must observe successes and failures. We take the best and then adjust and adapt, based on our situation.

We are also compelled to share our learning with others. Our successes and failures can serve as examples and encouragement. We can help others avoid mistakes that we have made, and we can help them be better than we were.

GOD HAS CALLED US TO BE IN COMMUNITY WITH OTHERS, AND THIS APPLIES TO LEADERS AS WELL.

For leaders, there is both opportunity and responsibility. God has called us to be in community with others, and this applies to leaders as well.

The denomination that I serve has three financial-service-related organizations—an employee benefits provider, a foundation, and a banking institution. Different organizations, different challenges, but similar missions.

The global financial crisis hit each of these organizations hard, as did the COVID-19 pandemic. The challenges we faced were similar but still different. Therefore, the solutions were similar yet at the same time unique. Any attempt to insert identical solutions would have been misguided and suboptimal, perhaps even disastrous.

It is a joy and privilege to meet with my counterparts at these entities regularly. The three CEOs are in many ways more different than the organizations we serve. Yet we connect often, learning from and sharing with one another. We ensure that our organizations are coordinating and complementing one another while acting according to our unique needs.

Most important, we strive to embody 1 Thessalonians 5:11: "Therefore encourage one another and build one another up, just as you are doing."

Figuring Things Out, but Not Making a Decision

Solving problems requires us to find and execute optimal solutions for our unique situations. But what happens when we neglect or avoid one of these steps?

As I discussed earlier, many of those with strong analytical skills and abilities can suffer from analysis paralysis. Having spent their academic careers being rewarded for finding the correct answer, they are confronted with a reality in life: a unique correct solution rarely, if ever, exists.

So, they continue to study the problem. They search for more data. They wait for more data points to occur so they can rerun the analysis. Fear takes over, and no decision is made.

Leaders must accept the fact that full, complete, and perfectly accurate data never exists in the real world. A decision must be made based upon what is known.

An even worse situation occurs when there is contradictory data. Analysis paralysis sends one on a quest to reconcile the contradictions. Once again, fear takes over.

Another form of analysis paralysis occurs when the data could take a person in two (or more) different directions. The data may not be contradictory per se, but depending on how it is interpreted or which data set is relied on, different courses of action would be taken. Here again, fear can take over.

Leadership is an art, not a science.

Gather and analyze as much information as possible. But, at some point, you have to act on what you have.

AT SOME POINT YOU HAVE TO ACT ON WHAT YOU HAVE.

Consider all the possibilities. Weigh the advantages and disadvantages. Identify and quantify the risks. Listen to many voices—especially those that are not in full alignment with your thinking.

Pray. Seek counsel. Listen. Pray some more. Make your decision.

Making a Decision
before Figuring Things Out

Years ago, there was a TV show that fully exposed the humorous side of the human condition. Long before everyone had cameras in their phones, people lugged around massive video cameras to capture key moments in life. People would send in video clips to this television program that would be bundled into a thirty-minute show.

Today, we have cell phones to capture the moments, and we have YouTube and social media to distribute those videos to the masses. It seems that the final words spoken prior to the start of many of these clips were "Here, hold my beer."

You do not have to look very hard to find moments when people chose to act before fully thinking through the situation.

These moments can bring great levity. Sometimes, however, they bring tragedy. We listen to news reports and wonder "What were they thinking?" Sometimes the consequences of one's decisions could not have been anticipated. Many times, however, the consequences should have been apparent.

As leaders, we are compelled to figure things out, to solve problems.

We must carefully look out our side windows to understand our environment. We must look in the rearview mirror to learn from our past. We must gather as much information as we can. We must listen to other voices, gain other perspectives, and seek wise counsel. Heed the advice given by King Solomon: "Where there is no guidance, a people falls, but in an abundance of counselors there is safety" (Proverbs 11:14).

Pray for wisdom and discernment and for God's will to be done. And then, as the leader, make the decision.

But don't stop there. It is not over at this point. We must act. More important, we must execute with excellence.

> **WE MUST ACT. MORE IMPORTANT, WE MUST EXECUTE WITH EXCELLENCE.**

Even if there were a playbook and we were able to call the right play based on all the factors, the team must still run the play. And if they do not run it correctly, none of the above matters. No ground will be gained. We might be tackled for a loss or, worse, turn the ball over.

All the time spent planning, analyzing, and strategizing is meaningless if we fail in the execution. Our job as leaders continues through this critical phase, ensuring that the team is working together to achieve the desired outcomes.

One final but important note: It is very likely that something will not go according to plan. And once again, as the leader, you will be called on to make it up as you go along.

Enjoy the journey!

CHAPTER 3

THE ILLUSION *of* ABSOLUTE AUTHORITY

I cannot prove it definitively, but I have observed an interesting correlation. If you talk with parents, you will find that their awareness of different movies and TV shows is highly correlated with the ages of their children or perhaps grandchildren. Having three sons born in the late 1980s and early 1990s, I am deeply aware of certain movies and shows. There are others that I have no clue as to what they are about, yet some parents (or grandparents) seem to know them very well.

Take from it what you will, but I have probably seen *The Lion King* 142 times. Maybe more if you count the times the DVD was played while we were driving to visit family in Nebraska or Minnesota. At one time, I probably could have recited the entire movie.

In thinking about this chapter, one song from *The Lion King* has been playing through my head. Although humorous, the song speaks directly to some of the immaturity of youth: the perception that things will be so much better when I am in charge.

In the song, Simba looks forward to the point in time when he will be king. (For those not familiar, Simba is a lion cub whose father happens to be the king. Although still young, Simba understands how royalty and lines of succession work, and he is anticipating his eventual reign over the kingdom.) He first relishes the fact that no one will tell him what to do, and as the song goes on, he takes it to a new level—one day he will be the one telling others what to do!

The Boss, but Not in Charge

I remember when my kids discovered that I was a boss. Their eyes opened wide as they thought through all the ramifications. They thought it was pretty cool that I got to tell people what to do! They had no idea.

Of course, what makes Simba's song hit home is that we all can relate to that immature view of leadership or of being in charge. Although we are not looking forward to a day when we will be king, we may have had similar thoughts at different points in our lives. I know I did.

Just wait until I am older . . .

Just wait until I am the parent . . .

Just wait until I am the boss . . .

Just wait . . . I will show you how it's done!

And then we get older, and we find that life was much easier when we were younger. We find out that nearly everything is more difficult and complicated than we could have ever imagined.

We become parents, and we realize how wise and patient our parents were.

We become the boss, and we quickly find out that it doesn't seem to work the way we thought it would.

Oh, I just couldn't wait to be king . . .

This book is not written for kings or dictators. I have no insights on how to do any of that stuff. Instead, this book is written to and for leaders. Kings and dictators may have absolute authority. For the rest of us, however, absolute authority is an illusion.

My kids thought that, as a boss, I had the sort of power Simba dreamed he would have one day. "No one tells my dad what to do; he is the boss!" "My dad is the boss; he tells everyone what to do!"

The reality, however, is quite different.

Even today, as president and CEO, I may be the boss, but I am not in charge!

As leaders, we are always accountable to someone else. First and foremost, we are accountable to our Creator and Redeemer. You and I have been called to our various vocations to serve others. We are stewards, not owners (even if you own your company). All that we have comes from the hand of our heavenly Father. Our time as stewards is but for a season. And then it will all be turned over to a new steward.

> I MAY BE THE BOSS, BUT
> I AM NOT IN CHARGE!

The writer of Ecclesiastes puts it this way:

> **I hated all my toil in which I toil under the sun, seeing that I must leave it to the man who will come after me, and who knows whether he will be wise or a fool? Yet he will be master of all for which I toiled and used my wisdom under the sun. This also is vanity.** (ECCLESIASTES 2:18–19)

Leadership is a bit like a relay. I received the baton from someone else, and now it is my turn to run. Eventually, I will hand the baton off to the one who follows me. My contribution to the team and to the race will be over. This is true for me as I serve a board of directors, and it is even true for those who own their business, as they will one day turn it over to someone else.

One of my jobs as a leader is to keep things moving. In this relay, it is imperative that I hold on to the baton. My next priority is to gain as much ground as I can. But, ultimately, I must ensure that the team does not lose ground that others will have to make up.

At this point, I may seem a little down on leadership or our roles as leaders. But please do not read any of this that way. The call to leadership is an honor and a privilege. It is incredibly humbling to consider the fact that God called me to this position and equipped me to serve His purposes. That decision was not made in 2008 when the board asked me to become CEO or even in 1962 when I was born. God had it in His plan from the beginning of time that I would be called to serve at this time in this way.

Likewise, you have been called. And that call was part of God's plan from the beginning. You are His chosen steward at this time and in the place and role that He has prepared for you and prepared you for!

He has called us to serve for a season, to run our race, and then to hand things off to those who follow. That person may be wise or foolish, but the future is in God's hands, not ours. We play our part. We trust God to do His!

THE FUTURE IS IN GOD'S HANDS, NOT OURS.

Gaining Perspective

The point of all this is to establish a proper perspective of our role as leaders. If your pursuit of leadership is to fulfill a desire to someday be the king, you are destined for failure. That failure will result from not understanding or fully appreciating two key leadership principles:

1. **You may be the boss, but you are not in charge.**

2. **Absolute authority is the absolute worst way to lead.**

We will dive into the topic of accountability more fully in the next chapter, but for now we must understand that Christian leaders are first and foremost accountable to God, the one who created us and calls us to serve in our various vocations. But we are accountable to others as well.

In my role as president and CEO, I am accountable to a board of directors. I honor and respect the authority they have over me. I serve the board and support them in fulfilling their responsibilities to the church-at-large. I serve as their hands and their voice in between their formal meetings. I provide advice and recommendations to them. I solve problems on their behalf. I serve at their pleasure.

I am accountable to The Lutheran Church—Missouri Synod, to the thousands of ministries that form the LCMS, and to the tens of thousands of church workers who serve faithfully.

I am accountable to the leaders of the LCMS and of its many ministries.

I am accountable to the employees of Concordia Plan Services.

I am accountable to my wife and to my family.

I am accountable to my friends and neighbors.

I might be the boss, but I certainly am not in charge.

Not unlike some of the dangers discussed in chapter 1, we face very real danger when we fool ourselves into thinking that we are actually in charge—the first misperception. We run the risk of putting ourselves into the role of God, rather than honoring Him as master and understanding our role as stewards.

The second misperception is what I am calling the illusion of absolute authority. While absolute authority exists, many people believe it's far more effective than it actually is.

The immature lion cub envisioned the grandeur of kingship. He saw the adoring masses bowing down. The entire kingdom would bend to his will.

Adults, too, buy into this illusion.

Consider the president of the United States. The president is seen as the leader of the free world, and certainly the commander in chief part of the job is very real. But even in this capacity, the president depends heavily on military and intelligence leaders for guidance and recommendations. The president is accountable for making the tough decisions, and from that standpoint has incredible power. Yet that power is still contained as matters rise through the ranks, and then action flows back out through those same channels.

Or take the legislative process in the United States. We tend to think that our political party could easily execute its goals if only it had more authority. But even if one party has control of the White House, the Senate, and the House, legislative agendas can be difficult to execute.

After spending time with members of congress and their staff, I learned a bit about how the sausage is made, so to speak.

Getting even noncontroversial measures to pass through both chambers can be an ordeal. Measures can fail simply because the other side does not want to give their opponent a win.

Recently, we saw this play out with Republicans, who for years campaigned on the promise to repeal and replace the Affordable Care Act. Yet, once they had the White House, the Senate, and the House, they were unable to fulfill their pledge. Everyone was supposedly on the same team, yet that team failed to bring forward a victory.

Absolute authority was but a mirage.

As employees, we can take the same perspective that Simba had: if I were the boss, here is how I would do things . . .

> **ABSOLUTE AUTHORITY WAS BUT A MIRAGE.**

As congregational members, we look at the pastor or the church council and think about how we would do it if we were in charge . . .

As parents, we question teachers and administrators, thinking of how we would do things if we were in charge . . .

Then, one day, we get promoted and take on a leadership role at work. Only then do we find out just how difficult it can be to manage people.

One day, we get elected to a position at our church, and we learn how difficult it is to balance so many competing perspectives.

One day, we join the school board and see how difficult it is to lead a school.

The illusion of absolute authority shatters.

Leadership roles bring challenges that others rarely see or appreciate. But it is the nature of the game.

It is easy to sit in the stands and think about how I would have played or coached the game differently. But I have no idea what things are like down on the field.

In my younger years, I was quick to judge the actions and decisions of others. Today I would like to think that I am more aware of all that I do not know. I do not know the full extent of the facts and circumstances my fellow leaders face. I do not have expertise with their business models. I do not understand the constraints they are under. And so I trust that they are making the best decisions they can, given all the circumstances and constraints they are facing. I trust that they know things I am not privy to. I trust that they understand their respective risks better than I do.

I also understand fully that they, like me, are not king.

Understanding the illusion of absolute authority in my role compels me to grant them grace. Moreover, if I truly believe that God has called me to be a leader at this time and in this place, then I must also trust God as He similarly called other leaders to their positions.

I wield the sword of absolute authority sparingly, and I trust other leaders to make their own leadership decisions. They do not know the full extent of the challenges I face, and I do not fully understand their context either.

Rather than judge or second guess, we should encourage, support, and lift up one another as we take on the roles and responsibilities of our respective calls.

Influential Authority

What, then, is the purpose of a president and CEO if absolute authority is an illusion?

Let me clarify: absolute authority exists. It is real. The illusion comes in the misperception of its role, function, and application.

As CEO, I have absolute authority within the parameters established by the board. But I am granted that authority to utilize for the sake of the organization, not for my own sake. It is a sword that comes with great responsibility, and therefore it must be used with great discretion. In fact, I pray I never have to use it.

Perhaps an example is helpful. We all know that parents have absolute authority over their children. Okay, parents, now that you are done laughing, let's dive into that point more deeply. Of course, there is an establishment of authority. But as powerful as you may be as a parent, absolute authority is useless against a strong-willed toddler. Absolute authority ends when the sixteen-year-old walks out the door with the car keys.

As our children grow and challenge our authority, there will be times when we have to play the parent card: "Because I am the parent, that's why!" Some situations require us to play that card of absolute authority. But seasoned parents know well that it must be used sparingly.

If you only rely on—or overly rely on—absolute authority, your time as a leader is destined for failure.

The most powerful form of authority is not absolute authority. That power fades quickly. Like a shot of adrenaline, its effect wears off, making you feel weaker when it is done.

Instead, the real power is found in influential authority.

> THE REAL POWER IS FOUND IN INFLUENTIAL AUTHORITY.

My lasting impact as a father or grandfather comes not by telling my children what to do. The lasting impact comes from what I model for them. Actions do, in fact, speak louder than words.

If I want my kids to go to church, I need to go to church. If I want my sons to treat their wives with respect, I need to treat their mother with respect. If I want my sons to be godly fathers, I need to show them what that looks like, as my dad did for me.

Speaking of Influence

The seed of this idea was first planted in my mind years before I became CEO. Having been exposed to the work of Jim Collins and his landmark book *Good to Great*, I was then introduced to a companion piece, *Good to Great and the Social Sectors*.[2] I highly recommend both books and would even say that the latter is mandatory reading if you are in the nonprofit space.

---

2   See Jim Collins, *Good to Great: Why Some Companies Make the Leap . . . and Others Don't* (New York: HarperCollins Publishers, 2001) and *Good to Great and the Social Sectors: Why Business Thinking Is Not the Answer* (New York: HarperCollins Publishers, 2005).

In the second piece, Collins explores and adapts his "good to great" concepts to the nonprofit world. Of particular interest is a chapter on leadership in the social sector called "Getting Things Done within a Diffuse Power Structure."

Many of my readers will be part of The Lutheran Church—Missouri Synod. Can there be a better case for an organization with a diffuse power structure? The same goes for congregations, schools, recognized service organizations, and other ministries within the denomination. It is true for civic groups and all other sorts of nonprofits as well. In these types of environments, absolute authority is rarely effective.

In my previous role as a vice president, I was responsible for supporting one of the committees of our board. The chair of that committee had a profound impact on me as I was growing and developing as a leader. When it was only he and I in the room, he would push and prod me. He would try to poke all sorts of holes in my proposals. He would challenge me continuously. But when we were in the committee meetings, he would support and defend me. He would ensure that the proposals moved through the committee and up to the board for approval. He gave me all the credit in public.

The lesson? Influence is the way to get things done. I had no authority in that setting. But if I could convince this committee leader of the merits of my proposal, the remainder of the process would be smooth sailing.

INFLUENCE IS THE WAY TO GET THINGS DONE.

Now, the process of convincing that committee leader was no simple task. It could take weeks and months to work through challenging proposals. I was the subordinate and he the superior. But I could ensure that much was accomplished if I worked to influence with humility.

Influence, not authority, is the key to getting things done in a diffuse power structure!

The Power of Influence

Absolute authority can certainly seem a lot easier and more effective. Unless you are an actual dictator, that perception is part of the illusion.

Influential authority does take work and it does take time. By nature, it is relational. It involves a strong element of trust.

Perhaps not a perfect application, but not inappropriate either—we are called in Matthew 5 to be salt of the earth and light to the world! To do so, we need to be involved and engaged, not distant.

> WE NEED TO BE INVOLVED AND ENGAGED, NOT DISTANT.

Christian leaders will recognize that influential leadership has biblical roots. While the following passage was written to a specific group of leaders, the apostle Peter clearly preferred influential authority over absolute authority and offered a compelling vision of leadership for us to reflect on:

> So I exhort the elders among you, as a fellow elder and a witness of the sufferings of Christ, as well as a partaker in the glory that is going to be revealed: shepherd the flock of God that is among you, exercising oversight, not under compulsion, but willingly, as God would have you; not for shameful gain, but eagerly; not domineering over those in your charge, but being examples to the flock. (1 PETER 5:1–3)

CHAPTER 4

THE ELUSIVENESS *of* ACCOUNTABILITY

I am a math guy. For me, mathematics has always come easily. The principles are absolute. There are definitions, and those definitions are unambiguous. Perhaps that is why I tended to struggle more in subjects such as spelling and English—the rules were not so absolute (and at times appeared to be arbitrary).

Words certainly do have meaning. But nearly every dictionary entry lists multiple definitions for a single word. Definitions can vary by context, or the definition can depend on one's perspective.

Take the word *hill*. Seems pretty simple, doesn't it? A hill is a hill. We all know what a hill is. But if you are running a distance race or out on a long bike ride, you may see something as a hill that others see as a moderately sloped grade. Having driven race routes prior to a half marathon, I can tell you that hills often appear on the route overnight!

ACCOUNTABILITY IS ONE OF THE MOST IMPORTANT ASPECTS OF LEADERSHIP.

Accountability is one of the most important aspects, if not perhaps *the* most important aspect, of leadership. It is a concept that is widely written and spoken about. Many speakers and authors focus on accountability. Yet it seems that accountability can be a bit nebulous or, as I have described it, elusive.

From a definition standpoint, *accountability* may seem straightforward. Various online dictionaries all center around a theme of accepting responsibility for one's actions.

So why is accountability so elusive?

One reason may be that accountability is less apparent when we watch events play out in real time; we are not always privy to the ways people have been held to account or taken responsibility. Conversely, lack of accountability surrounds us and fills the daily news. Examples of people avoiding accountability are often more obvious and abundant than those of people taking responsibility.

Many politicians shun any sort of accountability. There is little to no accounting for waste of government resources. There is no accounting for the lack of results. For decades, we have had wars on poverty, wars on drugs, and wars on terrorism. Yet poverty, drugs, and terrorism are still with us. Did we even make a dent? Are there any measurable results? Who is accountable for the wasted time and resources? Who is accountable for the human suffering that continues unabated?

We hear that billions of dollars were wasted in the name of COVID-19 relief. Some of the projects would be laughable if the neglect wasn't so great. After the first waves of relief dollars that focused on paycheck protection, what was actually accomplished?

We see a lack of accountability in the corporate sector as well. Boards and CEOs seem beyond being held to account for actions and results. Even when CEOs lose their positions, large payouts often walk out the door with them.

Rather than people stepping up and taking accountability for what happened (or did not happen), excuses and blame become a standard response. Actions often have no material consequences.

Lack of accountability is all around us. To make matters worse, that lack of accountability is too often rewarded. This happens when those who should be held accountable acts as though they are somehow victims of the circumstances.

Given its rarity, one might think true accountability would stand out and be rewarded all the more, that it would be identified and celebrated, promoted and encouraged.

ACCOUNTABILITY REMAINS ELUSIVE.

Instead, accountability remains elusive.

To get a better grasp on this important concept and why it is essential for Christian leaders, I will describe two types of accountability: retroactive accountability and proactive accountability. I will also address the dangers of fake accountability.

Retroactive Accountability

We are all too familiar with retroactive accountability. This is when one's past actions or results are reviewed after the fact. Human nature being what it is, people tend to despise or avoid such scrutiny.

During childhood, we regularly experienced such reviews—they were called report cards. There were always a few students who actually enjoyed receiving report cards, but most of us dreaded the day our parents would open the envelope and read our teacher's evaluation of our performance.

I don't know about you, but I was called to give explanations for what was reported by my teachers. And like most kids, I got pretty good at crafting explanations for whatever may have been on that report card. Of course, in my generation, what the teacher said carried more weight with my parents than any of my attempts to rationalize away a poor assessment.

As we grew older, the impact of those school reviews became more critical because they translated into our grade point average. That GPA often affected which schools we could attend and which companies would grant us job interviews. As we applied for schools and interviewed for positions, we had more opportunities to perfect our ability to provide an explanation for whatever those reviews revealed.

When we entered the working world, we stopped receiving report cards and instead began to experience some sort of annual performance appraisal. And we continued the trend of providing answers for the things we accomplish or failed to accomplish.

Retroactive accountability evaluates how we performed, or failed to perform, on a set of responsibilities or tasks. During our school years, the responsibilities took the form of assignments, papers, quizzes, tests, and so on. The evaluation was at times objective and at times subjective.

In the work world, our responsibilities are often defined by our job description (at least in theory). We are given certain tasks, and our boss provides a review that, again, may be objective or subjective. That is a common theme with retroactive accountability—the responsibilities or tasks are often given or assigned to us.

Done correctly, regular performance reviews can be valuable to the individual and to the organization. But the retroactive accountability of annual performance reviews is generally ineffective at driving results. In and of themselves, they do little to help people develop or achieve organizational goals.

Retroactive accountability tends to result in the blame game. Behaviors that were well honed during the school years come on display in the work world. Cries of "that was not my job" or "no one told me" resound. Finger-pointing (in all directions) ensues. Ownership is avoided at all costs.

> RETROACTIVE ACCOUNTABILITY TENDS TO RESULT IN THE BLAME GAME.

Retroactive accountability places the attention on the actions of a single person. Team or organizational performance becomes secondary. Imagine how this would play out on any sort of athletic team: "It doesn't matter that we lost. I did my job."

At a broader level, we often see the effects of retroactive accountability when something unfortunate happens. When a tragic event takes place, the media and others look for a scapegoat. The cry goes up that someone needs to be held accountable, and the blame game commences.

Certainly, the events leading up to a tragedy need to be investigated. That investigation may determine that someone was at fault, and that person may face consequences for any neglect or criminal activity. But the greater value of learning what happened and why is so that information can be used to avoid or prevent future tragedies.

Unfortunately, the media and political leaders are working other agendas. Retroactive accountability becomes a sword to serve other causes.

Lutheran Christians could interpret retroactive accountability as an instrument of the Law. The Law serves as a curb to keep us from doing wrong, as a mirror to show us our sin, and as a guide to show us how to live. But the Law cannot change hearts.

ACCOUNTABILITY IS ELUSIVE BECAUSE IT IS TOO OFTEN UNDERSTOOD AS SOMETHING NEGATIVE.

Accountability is elusive because it is too often understood as something negative. We tend to think only of retroactive accountability.

Accountability, as a key leadership trait, comes in the form of proactive accountability.

Proactive Accountability

With retroactive accountability, we look backward to see who *was* accountable. With proactive accountability, we focus on who *is* accountable.

Proactive accountability is a mindset. It comes from within and is driven by a sense of duty or obligation. As Christian leaders, proactive accountability stems from our understanding of vocation—that God has called and equipped us to serve in our various roles.

Retroactive accountability emanates from a responsibility or task that was assigned, and the motivation is primarily external. Proactive accountability is primarily internal.

THERE ARE KEY INDICATORS OF PROACTIVE ACCOUNTABILITY WE CAN LOOK FOR.

The internal nature of proactive accountability means that it defies measurement, which can contribute to the impression that accountability is elusive. However, there are key indicators of proactive accountability we can look for.

Because proactive accountability is a mindset, it does not require a title or formal role or delegated responsibility. Proactive accountability can appear when someone steps in to do the right thing for the right reason. Therefore, it can be found in a child on the playground who defends another child who is being picked on or invites someone to leave the sidelines and join a game.

Proactive accountability begins with an ownership mentality. As discussed previously, leaders are stewards, with God being the ultimate owner. But an ownership mentality does not require actual ownership. Instead, we adopt the perspective of the owner as we contemplate actions and make decisions.

The parable of the talents (Matthew 25:14–25) comes to mind here. Three servants were entrusted with a portion of the master's property, each according to his ability. Two servants provided a 200 percent return on the investment. We are not told how the returns were achieved, but the implication is strong: those two servants put the capital to work. They took risks, and they provided the master with the reward.

This stands in stark contrast to the third servant, who merely returned the one talent that he was given. Out of fear, he hid his talent away. He did not think or act as the master would have. In fact, he even attempted to pin the blame for his lack of results on the master himself (see verses 24–25)!

The first two servants took on an ownership mentality on behalf of the master. They put the assets to work on his behalf. They modeled proactive accountability.

An ownership mentality means we will focus on outcomes or results rather than actions or activities. A focus on activities (retroactive accountability) is evident with excuses like "I did my job." Proactive accountability is satisfied only when the desired outcomes are achieved.

Proactive accountability involves a recognition that commitments have been made to others, and it ensures that those commitments are met.

Of course, there are times when commitments cannot be honored despite our best efforts. Retroactive accountability would bring out excuses and identify scapegoats to blame. Proactive accountability, however, steps up and acknowledges the failure. The proactive leader accepts the blame and the consequence and looks for a path to rectify the situation to whatever extent is possible.

Proactive accountability allows for explanation of failure. There may be good and valid reasons why a particular endeavor failed. There is a big difference between providing *reasons* for the failure and providing *excuses* for the failure.

Excuses shift the blame. Reasons provide understanding.

PROACTIVE ACCOUNTABILITY LOOKS TO FIX PROBLEMS, NOT FIX THE BLAME.

Proactive accountability is driven to find and understand the reasons for the failure. Failures often provide more opportunities to learn, and much more valuable lessons, than successes.

Proactive accountability looks to fix problems, not fix the blame. Of course, there is a time and place for retroactive accountability. Depending on the nature of the failure and the decision-making process, corrective actions may need to be taken and someone may need to be held accountable. Just as there continues to be a need for the Law for those of us living under the Gospel, so proactive accountability does not remove the need for retroactive accountability. The primary focus, however, shifts to learning and correction, not punishment or blame.

As Christians, this fits beautifully with our understanding of forgiveness. We can identify and own our failures, and we can confess to God and to others our mistakes with the full assurance of forgiveness and restoration! Conversely, we see that fear, excuses, and finger-pointing all move us away from our Savior and from one another.

Proactive Accountability in Action

Did you know that 50 percent of all NFL teams fail each weekend? (The actual percentage may be a bit higher or lower depending on how you view ties!)

What is the focus in the postgame interviews discussing the loss? Officiating? Weather? Injuries?

You have to listen closely, as the officiating may be a legitimate reason, not an excuse. Same with the weather or injuries. These may just be the conditions that affected the outcome of a game. Are they presented as explanations or excuses?

A coach or player displays an ownership mentality by directly addressing the failings and the learnings that came with that failure. He or she takes direct and personal responsibility. Proactive accountability speaks to the upcoming week of practice and the commitment to make corrections before next week's game.

This lesson was taught to me when I was attending Concordia University, Nebraska back in the 1980s. On Sunday nights in the fall, I would watch the Tom Osborne Show. In one hour, you saw the complete Cornhuskers game from the day before, along with the legendary coach's commentary on every play from his team.

Whenever there was a failure, Coach Osborne would note that "we" didn't execute properly. That seemed a bit odd on things like a missed kick when the snap, the hold, and the blocking were perfect—it was pretty clear whose fault it was.

Yet on any good play, Coach Osborne would name the player or players who led to the success.

Coach Osborne made himself part of every failure but only pointed toward others in times of success.

The focus was always on learning and preparing for next week—to be better tomorrow than today. To give credit and take blame.

We have been considering leadership as a journey. As leaders, we need to ensure that the desired results are delivered—that the final destination is reached. Proactive accountability, then, must occur throughout the entire process.

> PROACTIVE ACCOUNTABILITY, THEN, MUST OCCUR THROUGHOUT THE ENTIRE PROCESS.

Imagine you set off on a road trip to southern California but instead found yourself in the state of Washington. Retroactive accountability would wait until you were in Seattle before demanding answers for how you got there; it would seek to identify who was at fault. However, proactive accountability would be at work throughout the trip—meaning that you never ended up in Seattle at all because course corrections were continually made along the way.

Before we had navigation apps on our phones, we had actual, physical maps. Prior to setting out on a cross-country journey, we would plot our course and note the various highways we would have to traverse. Inevitably, there would be delays and detours, perhaps some wrong turns. Without our electronic gadgets to instantly reroute us, we were the ones who had to correct our course.

Likewise, proactive accountability adjusts the plan as the situation warrants to achieve the desired outcomes. The route may be a bit different than what was originally planned due to detours, and the timeline may need to be extended to account for the additional miles driven, but the destination is ultimately reached!

Fake Accountability

Another reason accountability can be elusive is because of an imposter in the mix. That imposter might look and sound like accountability, but it lacks substance and character.

One way this imposter shows up is under the cloak of empowerment.

Please understand this: with true accountability, empowerment is a powerful force. But I am referring here to empowerment *without* accountability.

Many people will say that they want to be empowered. They will note that they should just be allowed to do something or manage a project without input or interference from others, be it bosses or peers. If left alone to do things their way, with them calling the shots, things would be so much better and more effective, they claim.

The proof comes, however, when projects fail to meet their intended targets. With fake accountability, the person who sought empowerment moves into a mode of making excuses or pointing fingers. Sometimes the person lets projects or initiatives die slow and quiet deaths, hoping no one will notice. Conversely, empowerment with proactive accountability puts the team on a pathway to achieve the agreed-upon outcomes.

Another form of fake accountability is the "I told you so" response. When things have not gone according to plan, this person chimes in with "See, I warned you" or "You should have listened to me" or "I told you so." The person may have seen potential threats at the start of the project, and perhaps even tried to say something at the time. But the fake accountability of "I told you so" serves only the self and not the mission or the team. Proactive accountability would have compelled that person to greater action or to speak more loudly when risks were perceived earlier in the endeavor. And as we discussed earlier, proactive accountability would look to learn from failures instead of looking to blame others.

Another way the imposter shows up is through rigid dedication to executing the plan, no matter how circumstances change. Fake accountability shows dogged determination to the agreed-upon plan that on the surface may seem commendable. But proactive accountability is committed to the outcome, not the plan. Real accountability brings corrective action to achieve the desired goal.

> PROACTIVE ACCOUNTABILITY IS COMMITTED TO THE OUTCOME, NOT THE PLAN.

The Accountable Leader

Retroactive accountability focuses on who *was* accountable. Proactive accountability looks to who *is* accountable. The accountable leader says, "I *am* accountable."

The accountable leader

- displays an ownership mentality.
- commits to the mission over the plan.
- focuses on outcomes over activities.
- makes the tough decisions.
- answers for the decisions made.
- makes corrections as needed to achieve the desired goals.
- is curious and learns continuously.
- provides reasons, not excuses.
- honors commitments.
- owns failures.
- is optimistic and hopeful.
- places the organization and the team ahead of the self.
- is transparent.
- builds trust.
- is bold and courageous.

Accountability does not need to be elusive. Understanding the forms that accountability takes is essential to its proper execution and implementation.

There is a time for retroactive accountability. It is a valuable and essential tool. But it is also limited in its ability to drive change. Leaders must hold themselves and others accountable for decisions made and actions taken.

There is no room in an organization for fake accountability. That imposter undercuts the team and negatively impacts its overall results. The imposter serves the self, not the organization.

Proactive accountability holds the real power to move organizations forward and to achieve great outcomes!

CHAPTER 5

ALONE
in the MIDDLE

. . . .

It's lonely at the top."

People often say this with respect to a CEO or president of a company, or perhaps to a small-business owner, but it applies in many other settings as well.

As a CEO, I report to a board of directors. A team of vice presidents reports to me. The very nature of the CEO position means that I have no peers within my organization.

The same thing is true for many pastors, particularly those who are called to a senior or sole pastor position. In these situations, the pastor answers to the congregation, and at times, to multiple boards. Even if there is an assistant or associate pastor, they do not hold the same role or the same responsibilities as the senior pastor.

Likewise, in a school setting, there is one leader who reports to the board. Titles may include principal, executive director, and headmaster. Whatever the title, this person reports singularly to a board and oversees the faculty and staff.

Now, this chapter is not a complaining session. I am not declaring anything to be unfair. There is also nothing wrong with the nature of these organizational structures. To the contrary, these structures are critical in establishing a single clear point of accountability.

But leaders must recognize and deal with this reality, especially those who are just coming into such a position.

Because the actual title varies by organization and by the roles and responsibilities of the top position, I will use the term "accountable executive" going forward.

Let's go back to the idea of things being lonely at the top. There are a variety of opinions on the sources or causes of this sense of loneliness.

LEADERS MUST RECOGNIZE AND DEAL WITH THIS REALITY.

Some lines of thought attribute it to the fact that successful or powerful people may find it difficult to relate to those who have experienced less success or who possess less power. Conversely, it may happen because other people find it difficult to approach those in powerful positions.

Other lines of thinking observe that some people seek access to successful and powerful people for personal gain. This can make people in top roles wary of those who want to get close to them, causing them to isolate themselves.

Some or all of this may be true. But I believe there is more to it. I believe the issue is structural.

The Middle of It All

The title of this chapter gives a clue as to how leaders can better understand this sense of loneliness. The loneliness does not occur because the accountable executive is at the top. Rather, it comes from the fact that CEOs, senior pastors, principals, and other types of accountable executives are not at the top of anything! We are in the middle. And because there is only one accountable executive, it will be, by nature, a lonely position.

Traditional organizational charts perpetuate this misconception. The typical org chart pictures the accountable executive at the top of a pyramid-like structure—the king of the hill. It often looks something like this:

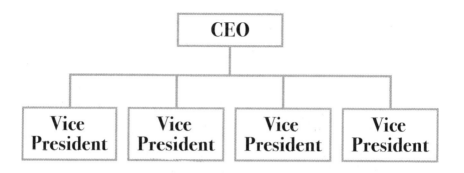

Oh, if only this were the case! What a view the CEO would have from that lofty perch—like the breathtaking vista that rewards those who hike to a mountain summit. The conquest is complete; time to sit back and enjoy the spoils.

In reality, the situation looks more like this:

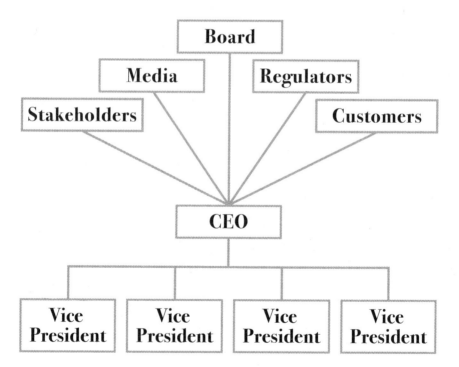

The accountable executive is found at the top of the traditional organizational chart while at the same time at the bottom of an inverted pyramid. That inverted pyramid funnels all the issues and pressures from on high to that single, solitary point of accountability.

Gone are any misconceptions about positioning; clearly, the accountable executive is not at the top. There is no mountaintop on which to relax—no clean, fresh mountain air to breathe, no looking down on the peaceful valley below. Instead, the executive faces a relentless flow of pressure coming down from multiple sources.

The accountable executive is firmly positioned in the middle. And it can be very lonely in the middle.

The Promise

If we truly believe that God has called us to be leaders in this time and in our respective roles, with our respective responsibilities, then we can be confident that He has prepared and equipped us to serve!

God knows that leadership is difficult. He knows that leadership positions can be lonely. One Old Testament account of leadership succession speaks directly to this matter.

GOD KNOWS THAT LEADERSHIP IS DIFFICULT.

At age 120, Moses turned over his role as leader of the people of Israel to Joshua. Moses knew something about being caught in the middle. He was called as the chosen leader of the people of Israel—the one to bring them out of captivity in Egypt and to the Promised Land.

Moses knew that Joshua would experience the loneliness of being in the middle. God knew it as well.

Speaking both directly to Joshua and through His prophet Moses, God gave Joshua instructions and words of encouragement. Note the repetition:

"Be strong and courageous. Do not fear or be in dread of them, for it is the LORD your God who goes with you. He will not leave you or forsake you." Then Moses summoned Joshua and said to him in the sight of all Israel, *"Be strong and courageous,* for you shall go with this people into the land that the LORD has sworn to their fathers to give them, and you shall put them in possession of it. It is the LORD who goes before you. He will be with you; He will not leave you or forsake you. Do not fear or be dismayed." (DEUTERONOMY 31:6–8, EMPHASIS ADDED)

And the LORD commissioned Joshua the son of Nun and said, *"Be strong and courageous,* for you shall bring the people of Israel into the land that I swore to give them. I will be with you." (DEUTERONOMY 31:23, EMPHASIS ADDED)

The LORD said to Joshua . . . , "No man shall be able to stand before you all the days of your life. Just as I was with Moses, so I will be with you. I will not leave you or forsake you. *Be strong and courageous,* for you shall cause this people to inherit the land that I swore to their fathers to give them. Only *be strong and very courageous,* being careful to do according to all the law that Moses My servant commanded you. . . . Have I not commanded you? *Be strong and courageous.* Do not be frightened, and do not be dismayed, for the LORD your God is with you wherever you go." (JOSHUA 1:1, 5–7, 9, EMPHASIS ADDED)

Like Joshua, you and I have been called by God to lead. He has commissioned us for service. He has prepared and equipped us to take on the roles and responsibilities that are placed in front of us. He has called you and I as leaders to be strong and courageous, even very courageous!

Joshua was about to be in the middle, just as Moses had been. As leaders, we are also in the middle. But thanks be to God, we are not alone.

God's promise to Joshua is also a promise He makes to you and me as leaders:

- He goes with you!
- He is with you!
- He will not leave you!
- He will not forsake you!

AS LEADERS, WE ARE ALSO IN THE MIDDLE. BUT THANKS BE TO GOD, WE ARE NOT ALONE.

Let that repetition sink in. The message is being reinforced for a reason: leadership is hard. True leadership requires strength and courage. The easy way out is often the route that does not require courage. Bold action is difficult. Bold action can often be misunderstood and unpopular.

That is why politicians often kick the can down the road and let those who follow deal with the growing challenges. No one taking a serious look at Social Security or Medicare can argue with the fact that these programs are woefully underfunded. Yet no politician, in either party, is willing to put forward a bold or courageous plan of action to correct the situation and get the programs onto a path of solvency. To do so would mean shattering any hope of reelection.

Likewise, our country needs rational immigration policies. Keeping everyone out doesn't work, and neither does letting everyone in. Real solutions require bold and courageous leadership.

REAL SOLUTIONS REQUIRE BOLD AND COURAGEOUS LEADERSHIP.

Neighborhoods are being torn apart by crime, drugs, and failing educational systems. Many local leaders are boldly and courageously making a difference in their communities, but we lack lasting solutions at the national or state level.

Are you a leader? Then be strong! Be courageous! Be the accountable executive you have been called to be.

Let God's word of promise encourage you today: He is with you. He will never forsake you!

The reality of our position in the middle does not go away. But by faith, we can lead with confidence, knowing that although it may feel lonely in the middle, we are not alone.

Wait for the Lord

King David was a man after God's own heart, yet he had his own struggles and challenges during his leadership journey. There had to have been times when he felt alone in the middle. In Psalm 27, David observed the evildoers looking to assail him (v. 2) and an army encamped against him (v. 3). His family had turned against him (v. 10). Yet his hope and confidence were in the Lord! David declared,

- "The Lord is my light and my salvation" (v. 1).

- "The Lord is the stronghold of my life" (v. 1).

- "He will hide me in His shelter in the day of trouble ... [and] lift me high upon a rock" (v. 5).

He then concluded, "I believe that I shall look upon the goodness of the Lord in the land of the living! Wait for the Lord; be strong, and let your heart take courage; wait for the Lord!" (vv. 13–14).

Once again, we hear those words of encouragement that were spoken to Joshua: Be strong! Take courage!

The Gift of Other People

In addition to the assurance of His presence, God also gives us the gift of other people to provide further support and encouragement. Although it may seem lonely in the middle, we are not alone.

I am blessed with an incredible, godly wife who has supported and encouraged me throughout my career and during my leadership journey. The blessings of family continue with our sons, daughters-in-law, and grandchildren. Home and family provide a needed respite and refuge from the day's challenges.

At the start of my career as an actuary, I was blessed to have a great boss. We did develop a friendship of sorts, but ever and always he was my boss. One of the many leadership lessons that I learned from Bill was that bosses, while not friends, could be allies and advocates. He would guide, encourage, and educate, yet still provide a strong dose of accountability when needed.

As the accountable executive in an organization, you likely do not have a single boss but instead report to a board. With a proper understanding of roles and responsibilities and a shared commitment to the mission of an organization, good board members can serve as allies and advocates for you as CEO.

During my yearslong tenure as CEO, I have been blessed with some great board members and great board chairs.

These people are resources that God has given you. When this system is executed properly, those people can help keep you from feeling alone in the middle.

The best resource on this topic is the book *The CEO and the Board: The Art of Nonprofit Governance as a Competitive Advantage*, written by my friend Dr. Kurt Senske.[3] I highly recommend this book to all leaders! Investing in and cultivating the right relationship between the board and the accountable executive pays incredible and invaluable dividends to the people involved, to the organization, and to those they serve.

Properly understood and executed, the relationship between the board chair and the accountable executive can be an incredible catalyst for increasing leadership effectiveness, which leads to greater organizational impact!

. . . .

3   See Kurt Senske, *The CEO and the Board: The Art of Nonprofit Governance as a Competitive Advantage* (St. Louis: Concordia Publishing House, 2023).

Early in my time as CEO, one board member (who was soon to become chair) encouraged me to get involved with some sort of executives' group. One recommendation was the Young Presidents' Organization. Unfortunately, I was six months too old to be considered a young president! But there were other groups and organizations for me to consider.

Through a variety of circumstances, God brought me to an organization called Vistage[4] and an outstanding group of local presidents, CEOs, and business owners. I was blessed to land in a St. Louis group that was led by one of Vistage's top chairs—he regularly received national honors for his exceptional work.

My group had fifteen to eighteen members, representing a variety of industries. Our business models and challenges were different, but we were all accountable executives, alone in the middle. A few answered to boards, as I did, some to private equity partners, and some to family members. But we each served as that single point of accountability in our organizations.

I SOON FOUND SUPPORT AND ENCOURAGEMENT BEYOND ANYTHING I COULD HAVE IMAGINED.

I will be honest—I was a bit overwhelmed coming into such an incredible group of leaders. But I soon found support and encouragement beyond anything I could have imagined. One group member served on the board of directors of the Missouri District of the LCMS. Another was a lifelong member of an LCMS congregation and had sent his children through Lutheran schools. A third was not Lutheran but ended up sending his children to Lutheran schools as well. These three had a personal, vested interest in my success as a CEO!

The Vistage chair and my fellow group members were instrumental in my growth and development as a CEO. I am tremendously grateful for all they did for me. Most of all, they helped keep me from feeling alone in the middle.

4   To learn more, go to www.vistage.com.

An organization like Vistage may not be the right fit for you. But I encourage you to find or create your own group of leaders to meet with regularly. Be open and transparent with one another, and "bear one another's burdens" (Galatians 6:2). Not only will they be a blessing to you, but you will also be a blessing to them on their leadership journeys!

Sharing the Burden

It is not uncommon for some to view delegation as merely the boss dumping the worst assignments on those reporting to them. Delegation, properly understood and executed, is so much more. It can lead to increased efficiency and effectiveness, which translates to superior results for the organization.

Consider again the organizational chart illustration earlier in the chapter. One might view this as a chain of command, and from an accountability perspective, that may be appropriate. But the bottom half of the chart creates a pyramid. The lower tiers of a pyramid are critical components of the structure; they provide support and stability for the whole. Likewise for leaders, those levels play a crucial role in achieving organizational support.

My board of directors provides me the resources (in other words, a budget) to assist in achieving the objectives of the organization. Delegation, properly understood, is a mechanism for sharing the burden!

The concept of delegation becomes even more powerful when we see it as a gift from God for His people. Simply put, delegation is also a biblical concept!

Consider an example from the early church. In Acts 6, there was a dispute going on with respect to a social ministry within the growing church. Rather than leaving their ministry of the Word, the apostles appointed what today we might call a committee (or even a board of directors) to oversee the care of widows. The committee was made up of individuals who were of good repute and full of the Spirit of God. Those were the criteria for who could be appointed to the committee; the job was not given to just anyone.

As a result, "the word of God continued to increase, and the number of disciples multiplied greatly" (Acts 6:7).

DELEGATION LEADS TO INCREASED MISSION EFFECTIVENESS.

Delegation leads to increased mission effectiveness.

Another example from the life of Moses further illuminates the wisdom of delegation for leaders in the middle. In Exodus 18, Moses was overwhelmed by the heavy burden of leadership, and his father-in-law, Jethro, shared invaluable advice:

> The next day Moses sat to judge the people, and the people stood around Moses from morning till evening. When Moses' father-in-law saw all that he was doing for the people, he said, "What is this that you are doing for the people? *Why do you sit alone, and all the people stand around you from morning till evening?*" And Moses said to his father-in-law, "Because the people come to me to inquire of God; when they have a dispute, they come to me and I decide between one person and another, and I make them know the statutes of God and His laws." Moses' father-in-law said to him, "*What you are doing is not good. You and the people with you will certainly wear yourselves out, for the thing is too heavy for you. You are not able to do it alone.* Now obey my voice; I will give you advice, and God be with you! You shall represent the people before God and bring their cases to God, and you shall warn them about the statutes and the laws, and make them know the way in which they must walk and what they must do. Moreover, *look for able men from all the people, men who fear God, who are trustworthy and hate a bribe, and place such men over the people as chiefs of thousands, of hundreds, of fifties, and of tens. And let them judge the people at all times. Every great matter they shall bring to you, but any small matter they shall decide*

themselves. So it will be easier for you, and they will bear the burden with you. If you do this, God will direct you, you will be able to endure, and all this people also will go to their place in peace." **So Moses listened to the voice of his father-in-law and did all that he had said.** (EXODUS 18:13–24, EMPHASIS ADDED)

Jethro was a wise man. Moses was not able to do it all by himself. He needed to appoint qualified individuals to share the burden. Note that Moses was not to delegate away the hardest decisions. As the accountable leader, he needed to be responsible for tough calls.

Look at the blessings Jethro identified:

- **It will be easier for you.**

- **They will bear the burden with you.**

- **God will direct you.**

- **You will endure.**

- **The people will go to their place in peace.**

The benefits of proper delegation bless not only the leader but also those whom the leader serves! And the leader's journey becomes sustainable—one that can be endured.

As leaders, we know the journey is hard. But God promises to be with us and to never leave us, and He also provides people to support and encourage us along the way.

As leaders, we are caught in the middle, but we are never alone.

Thanks be to God!

> AS LEADERS, WE ARE CAUGHT IN THE MIDDLE, BUT WE ARE NEVER ALONE.

PART 2

Getting Things Done

As we discussed in part 1, leaders are ultimately called to get things done. Stakeholder groups engage with your organization for a reason. There is an expectation of results. Even in the nonprofit realm, there is an expectation that outcomes will be delivered.

When I was young, the neighborhood guys and I would play all sorts of pickup games. Baseball, football, basketball, tennis, made-up games—you name it and we probably played it! Our choice of sports varied, with the biggest determining factor often being the number of guys present.

We would improvise greatly on the rules or parameters of the playing field to accommodate all sorts of factors. One of our regular football fields was at a local elementary school. Two parallel sidewalks made for the end zones. The sidewalk along the street was one sideline and the school building itself made up the other. Two spruce trees were part of the field of play, and they were used extensively to set picks on defenders.

These were, of course, not real games—just fun activities. Results didn't matter.

Unstructured play has real value when we are young. In addition to physical activity, it provides many opportunities for learning. We had to learn to work things out without referees, for example. We had to develop strategies on our own without the benefit of coaches.

I enjoy watching the kids in my neighborhood engage in similar activities. The peak of such activities was a few years ago. The gang of neighborhood boys was old enough for competitive play but too young for summer jobs and other such things. For a couple of summers, backyard baseball was the big event. They would play for hours, and my wife and I enjoyed spectating from a few backyards over.

Conflict inevitably arose (typically between brothers), but they always seemed to work things out. You could see the peacemakers step up to resolve conflict and get the game back on track.

But at the end of the day, these were activities, not real games.

Many people approach their work as if it were merely an activity. For them, work is an extension of the unstructured activities of youth. Show up, get a paycheck, go home. A job is merely something you do. Like the days on the playground, there is no desire for referees or coaches—just leave us alone to do our thing. No need for rules or regulations, we will handle things ourselves.

For leaders and those aspiring to be leaders, such an outlook is completely unacceptable.

Organizations exist for a reason. There is a mission; there is a purpose. There are expectations of results or outcomes of some sort.

In the for-profit world, one common metric serves as a great equalizer: profit. There can be different goals with respect to short-term or long-term profit. There can be different goals with respect to generating cash flow or building value. But success is ultimately determined by financial measurements.

For those of us in the nonprofit world, financial metrics are equally important, although for different reasons. The phrase "no margin, no mission" spells out the financial imperative clearly.

Nonprofit leaders cannot shirk their responsibility to be good stewards.

The ultimate objective for nonprofits, however, is not defined in terms of dollars. Nonprofits are evaluated on their effectiveness and efficiency in fulfilling their mission.

Nonprofits exist to positively impact the lives of people and to make society a better place.

Regardless of the setting, leaders are called to achieve results. Stakeholders have expectations of certain outcomes, and leaders must see that those expectations are met.

Leaders ensure that things get done. More to the point: leaders ensure that the right things get done and that they get done the right way.

To use the language of sports, it is not enough to simply play the game. Nor is it enough to play the game well. Coaches strive to win the game and ultimately win the championship. It is no longer play for the sake of play, as it was in the days of our youth. However you define winning in your setting, your job as leader is to bring home the "W".

Nonprofit organizations are defined by their mission. Results, then, are evaluated with respect to the completion of that mission.

Some argue that missions should be obtainable; others argue that they should be aspirational. Either way, they should provide clarity of purpose. They should form a basis by which leaders are ultimately evaluated.

Obtaining results is not always easy. Desired outcomes are not always achievable.

In the world of sports, every head coach has a counterpart across the field working to thwart every strategy thrown at him or her. Only one coach will win the game. Only one coach will win the championship.

There may not be an opposing coach countering every move you make as a leader, but there are other environmental factors at play.

Nonprofits do have competitors. The competition may not be in terms of products or services provided, but they may be competitors in terms of financial resources. Donors tend to favor organizations that demonstrate results with respect to mission.

Nonprofits are impacted by the economy—good or bad. Nonprofits can fall under regulatory scrutiny. Stakeholders are not always aligned.

Nonprofit leaders must be nimble in their approach. They must be able to adjust the game plan to achieve the desired outcomes.

In part 2, we will focus on ways of getting things done, of achieving results.

And while the lessons here are ones that were impactful for me in my leadership journey, the principles can apply to all sorts of situations.

CHAPTER 6

LEADERSHIP THROUGH TIMES *of* CRISIS

A Swedish proverb states, "Rough waters are a truer test of leadership. In calm water, every ship has a good captain." I have never attempted to captain a ship, but I do have some experience with boats, kayaks, and canoes. Most of those experiences occurred when conditions were fair. In my younger years, however, I spent a lot of time in northern Minnesota, canoeing in the Boundary Waters Canoe Area Wilderness. The BWCA is a remote wilderness area adjacent to the Canadian border. The ventures were weeklong trips, and the journey continued regardless of the conditions.

During the summer before my senior year of high school, I worked as a guide for an outfitter. We would take church youth groups and groups of troubled teens on trips into the BWCA. It was a pretty great summer job, as I got paid to canoe and camp. But it came with great responsibility—more than I understood or appreciated at the time.

Weeks with good weather were a piece of cake. Canoeing was relatively easy. Dry weather meant that setting up and breaking down camp was straightforward. Firewood was dry, making campfire cooking much easier.

But when the weather turned, everything was more difficult. There were days when we needed to make progress on our journey despite the weather conditions. Navigating a heavily laden canoe across a wide-open lake with even moderate winds is no easy task. The challenges increased as conditions worsened.

Different character traits became quite evident within our groups. Some people would rise to the challenge. Some simply endured. Some complained unceasingly.

But driving onward to the destination was the only option.

These memories give me a glimpse into the wisdom of the quote above. During good weather, the trips were more of a vacation. Adverse weather conditions, however, changed everything.

Rough waters create leaders. Rough waters allow for leadership skills to be honed. Rough waters differentiate levels of leaders. Rough waters prepare you for full-blown storms. Rough waters develop resilient leaders.

> ROUGH WATERS CREATE LEADERS.

Think of some people you consider to be great leaders. Did they have to navigate some sort of storm? Was it the storm, in fact, that defined them as leaders?

I think of great leaders such as George Washington, Abraham Lincoln, Winston Churchill, and Dwight D. Eisenhower. Each was tested by war, and not small wars either.

The truest tests of leadership come with adversity and times of crisis.

A Résumé of Leading during a Crisis

My tenure as CEO began in March of 2008. The organization I was asked to lead manages the employee benefits plans of The Lutheran Church—Missouri Synod. Our product portfolio included both defined benefit and defined contribution retirement plans, a comprehensive health plan, and disability and death benefits. At that time, we had approximately $3 billion of assets under management.

Less than a year later, we were in the midst of the Global Financial Crisis. In a matter of weeks, the value of the retirement plan assets dropped by $1 billion. Arithmetic can be brutal—a 33 percent loss requires a 50 percent recovery.

Not only was the United States facing the greatest economic challenge since the Great Depression but the entire world was thrust into the economic chaos as well, and the road to recovery was long. From an investment standpoint, there was nowhere to turn for safety.

What a welcome to the world of leadership!

Although I was the right-hand man to my predecessor for a number of years prior to becoming CEO, nothing prepared me for the storm we were facing.

NOTHING PREPARED ME FOR THE STORM WE WERE FACING.

Then in March of 2010, even as we still faced the fallout from the financial crisis, another form of crisis emerged. Via a budget reconciliation process, congress approved the Affordable Care Act, which President Obama quickly signed.

Because our organization provides a comprehensive health plan for the benefit of the ministries and workers of the LCMS, the Affordable Care Act brought us many more challenges—the first being requirements to provide coverages that were in direct conflict with our denomination's beliefs. The ACA also mandated that all individuals be covered by a qualifying health plan, but our plans could not qualify without compromising on our beliefs. The new standards for qualification crossed an important line with respect to religious freedom. Entities such as Hobby Lobby and Little Sisters of the Poor fought—and won—significant legal battles regarding the free exercise of faith. But those legal victories took years to make their way through lower courts.

Another threat embedded in the ACA gave us great cause for concern. The ACA would provide financial incentives (subsidies) for small employers—which includes the vast majority of LCMS ministries—to no longer offer health care as part of their employee benefit package and instead send their workers to the soon-to-be-created healthcare exchanges.

The plan for the ACA was in the works as early as 2008—before President Obama was even elected. On Inauguration Day in 2009, I was in Florida meeting with my counterparts from the benefit organizations of other denominations. Our Washington,

DC–based legislative counsel outlined the healthcare reform plan supported by President Obama.

Everyone in the room was stunned as we heard the plan. One of my colleagues said somberly, "So what you are saying is that we are all out of the business of providing health care."

Our DC-based friend replied simply: "Yes."

Good, bad, or otherwise, the Obama administration failed to efficiently and effectively implement the massive new law. State-based exchanges floundered. Lawsuits ensued. Inept leadership at the federal level kept the ACA from becoming what it was intended to be. The superstorm I and my counterparts feared never materialized, but it was and continues to be damaging, nonetheless.

Just two years into my tenure, the Global Financial Crisis landed a substantial blow to our retirement programs, and the Affordable Care Act had our health plan in its crosshairs, challenging not only our business model but also, and more importantly, the free exercise of our faith.

WHAT SORT OF CAPTAIN WAS AT THE HELM?

But if rough waters are true tests of leadership, what sort of captain was at the helm?

That captain had taken no courses on navigating a global financial crisis, nor had he any training on combating an attempted government takeover of health care. I don't remember those courses being offered as electives, either! I had no way to prepare for these tests—no textbooks to quote or algorithms to apply.

Those storms came early in my time as CEO, but more fun was in store.

Twelve years in and now a seasoned captain, I suppose, I was at the helm during a global pandemic. In a matter of weeks, we went from hearing about a virus spreading in China to shutting down our economy and keeping everyone at home and behind closed doors.

Once again, I do not recall anyone offering a class on leading an organization through a pandemic. The captain had never seen this type of storm before. And once again, I was unprepared for this test.

In addition to these challenges from the outside, we also face internal challenges.

By nature, the organization I serve could be considered a financial service organization. Any organization of this type relies on the law of large numbers. Larger customer bases and larger asset pools drive market efficiencies. For actuaries, the job gets easier as the base gets larger. Demographic trends become critical success factors.

Church membership across all mainline denominations, including the LCMS, has been in decline. Ministries close or dwindle. The pipeline of professional church workers is shrinking. In recent years, we have lost several of our denominational universities.

Thanks be to God that many of our Lutheran elementary and high schools are growing and even thriving in the post-pandemic world. But while those schools are attracting students, many are also finding it hard to attract and retain the teachers and staff needed to support the growth.

Demographic challenges may not be a full-fledged storm, but they are creating significant headwinds.

One thing is sure: this leadership journey is no pleasure cruise!

Finding the Path Forward

Every crisis is different in nature, in scope, and in magnitude. Every leadership journey is unique. Therefore, we will never find an exact checklist or procedure to navigate challenging times. However, I have learned through these experiences that certain leadership principles can be applied in any such circumstance.

CLARITY

At all times, but especially during times of crisis, leaders must provide clarity. People need to be reminded of the mission of the organization. For leaders navigating a crisis, organizational values become essential guideposts and norms for how to meet those challenges.

During the Global Financial Crisis, we were facing significant risks with respect to the future health and viability of the retirement programs we managed. Clarity of mission was essential for charting the path forward. We developed statements—not merely marketing talking points—that served as strategic imperatives to guide our decisions and actions.

Our two clarifying statements centered around preserving the core and sustaining the future.

> **CLARITY OF MISSION WAS ESSENTIAL FOR CHARTING THE PATH FORWARD.**

Over the years, our retirement programs had accumulated many extra features. Some of these were in the form of supplemental benefits, added at a time of excess funding. During times of plenty, the additions made sense. During lean times, however, it was essential that we preserve the traditional, core benefit.

Ultimately, the retirement programs needed to be restored to long-term financial viability. The Global Financial Crisis was broad and deep in impact, and the recovery was much slower than it had been with prior recessions. Every year of slow economic recovery following the initial crash added to the long-term challenges. Unlike Congress, our board and leadership team refused to kick the proverbial can down the road for someone to fix later.

These two statements provided clarity, and the clarity was aligned with and in full support of our mission. These statements were congruent with our organization values. These statements did not, however, tell us what to do.

When leaders provide clarity, they are not telling people what to do. Rather, they are painting a picture of the desired end state and providing guide rails for the journey.

People look to leaders to provide clarity during times of crisis.

At the outset of the global pandemic, I established two statements to guide how we would navigate those early days, weeks, and months. We committed to these two things:

1. **Keep the team safe.**

2. **Get the work done.**

We knew very little about COVID in March of 2020. Misinformation and fear were all around us. I wanted my team to know that our leadership team and I were committed to keeping people safe. We also understood that people needed to *feel* safe. This was a time to extend Christian care and compassion to others as we plotted our path forward.

We also had to commit to getting our work done. Ministries and members were counting on us to somehow do our jobs. If we expected them to continue to pay the bills, then we needed to continue to provide benefits and services.

These two guiding principles were not debatable; they just made sense. After clearly articulating our commitment to safety, our teams went to work figuring out how the work was going to get done.

As leader, I needed to provide clarity—not to prescribe what needed to be done, but to provide direction and ensure alignment.

COMMUNICATION

During times of crisis, leaders must also communicate regularly with both those inside the organization and external stakeholders.

Having established clarity of mission and purpose, we must reinforce it by repeating those key messages. It is simply impossible to overcommunicate during times of crisis. Even if it were possible to overcommunicate, it would have no negative consequences. Undercommunication, on the other hand, has significant negative consequences.

Communication also creates a sense of connection. That connection is important even when there are no storms, but it becomes critical when challenges arise.

IT IS SIMPLY IMPOSSIBLE TO OVERCOMMUNICATE DURING TIMES OF CRISIS.

The pandemic highlighted the value of communication. When we were forced to work remotely, I established a pattern of sharing a weekly email with our employees.

The weekly messages took on different forms. At times, I wanted to provide that clarity of purpose and mission to help keep us fully focused and aligned. At other times, I shared stories of how

I and others were navigating the pandemic to build connection. The messages emphasized that we were all in it together and encouraged us to "bear one another's burdens," along the lines of Galatians 6:2.

FOCUS

Another leadership principle for times of crisis is focus. A severe storm brings a lot of noise—thunder, rain, wind, hail, and so on. The noise can be frightening. The noise can be distracting and overwhelming. But the noise itself is not the problem. Leaders need to tune out the noise and center their focus on the most pressing issues.

Once we have clarity of mission and purpose, leaders must focus attention on what needs to be done now, in the moment. Elements of the annual plan may need to go out the window. Priorities that made sense in calm weather may no longer be priorities. Perhaps it is better to say that new initiatives overtake the planned activities.

For example, creating a remote workforce was not a priority for our organization in February 2020. By the end of March, it became one of our greatest priorities.

Leaders must help the organization focus on what is most important in the moment.

> LEADERS MUST FOCUS ATTENTION ON WHAT NEEDS TO BE DONE NOW.

PERSEVERANCE

Leadership is for the long haul. It is a marathon, not a sprint. In times of crisis, the burdens seem to grow exponentially, not just linearly. The length of the journey also increases.

During these times, people understandably grow weary. Leaders grow weary.

Training for a marathon is much more difficult than running a marathon. The marathon itself comes with a certain energy. Supporters line the race route. The other runners encourage one another. The atmosphere is energizing.

On those final training runs, however, there are no cheering crowds. No one to help pick you up mentally. You are alone with your aches and pains, your inner voice casting doubts about your abilities.

But it is through those long training runs that you develop the stamina to persevere. You train your body to endure the punishment and your mind to overcome the doubts.

It is okay for the leader to become weary and for others to see that occasionally. It is a reminder to everyone that leaders, too, have struggles and challenges.

But people also see the leader persevere.

CHRISTIAN LEADERS CAN BUILD SPIRITUAL DISCIPLINES THAT ENABLE THEM TO PERSEVERE THROUGH CHALLENGES.

Christian leaders can build spiritual disciplines that enable them to persevere through challenges. As with training for a marathon, those disciplines serve best if they are practiced in advance!

Reading God's Word, coming regularly to the altar to receive Holy Communion, being in fellowship with other Christians—these all fortify the body and soul for the challenges Christian leaders face.

FAITH

A time of crisis can create a sense of doubt in the mind of the leader. As others look to the leader for clarity and direction, the leader's internal voices cast shadows of doubt and uncertainty.

Frankly, I do not know where people turn if they do not have the hope and confidence found in our Lord and Savior, Jesus Christ. Without the certainty that all is in the hands of our loving Father, leaders can see themselves as the only one on whom everything depends.

But in times of crisis, Christian leaders can point others to the source of true hope and comfort. God has called and equipped us for the challenges in front of us. Rather than a rallying cry of "Follow me," Christian leaders encourage others to look to Jesus:

Therefore, since we are surrounded by so great a cloud of witnesses, let us also lay aside every weight, and sin which clings so closely, and let us run with endurance the race that is set before us, looking to Jesus, the founder and perfecter of our faith, who for the joy that was set before Him endured the cross, despising the shame, and is seated at the right hand of the throne of God. (HEBREWS 12:1–2)

For Christians and Christian leaders, faith is not just a way of getting through challenging times. Our faith is the foundation for all that we do!

> OUR FAITH IS THE FOUNDATION FOR ALL THAT WE DO!

OPTIMISM

Because of Jesus, and because we know that our heavenly Father has called us to be leaders, we can and must project optimism during times of crisis.

We are not optimistic because we have the answers. We are not optimistic because we know how everything will turn out. We, as leaders, do not have all the answers, nor do we know how things will turn out.

Likewise, our optimism is not foolishness or folly. We are not oblivious to the storms raging about us. The storms may do very real damage; severe storms typically do. Leaders need to be realistic and, more important, demonstrate that they are aware of and dealing with the reality of the situation.

During challenging times, the leader must project optimism, but that optimism must be grounded. It must be believable.

That is where Christian leaders have a distinct advantage: we get to share and give reason for the hope that is within us! (See 1 Peter 3:15.) When we lead by faith, we do so with full confidence in the One who has called and equipped us for the challenges we face. And we have the assurance that He will never leave us or forsake us!

Rising to the Challenge(s)

The words of Mordecai to Queen Esther run through my mind quite often: "Who knows whether you have not come to the kingdom for such a time as this?" (Esther 4:14).

Do I really, truly, deeply believe all that we say we believe about God? That He is all powerful and all knowing? That it has been His plan for all time that I would serve Him and His people in this time and place? Because if I do, then I believe that He has called and prepared me for the tasks at hand. And I must, then, believe that He has put me into this role for such as time as this.

He has placed me at the helm of this ship, knowing what storms are blowing up and what storms are yet to show themselves. By the grace of God, and by His provision, as leader I must navigate this ship and crew to safety.

> BY THE GRACE OF GOD, AND BY HIS PROVISION, AS LEADER I MUST NAVIGATE THIS SHIP AND CREW TO SAFETY.

I also think back to the words spoken to Joshua: Be strong. Be courageous. God is with me—He will never leave me or forsake me!

Although not a movie fanatic, I do have my favorite movie quotes. As I consider the magnitude of the challenges involved in leadership, I can't help but think of the great line delivered by Tom Hanks in *A League of Their Own*. Hanks's character, Jimmy Dugan, states, "Of course it's hard. It's supposed to be hard. If it was easy, everyone would do it. Hard is what makes it great."[5]

Leadership is hard. It is supposed to be hard. That is what makes it great!

If you are an emerging leader, I encourage you to examine yourself to see if you are truly up to the challenge. You do not need to have all the answers or any sort of special wisdom to take on leadership responsibilities. However, you do need the

5 *A League of Their Own*, directed by Penny Marshall (1992; Culver City, CA: Columbia Pictures, 1993), Laserdisc.

intestinal fortitude to face challenges and discover the embedded opportunities.

Returning to that great philosopher Jimmy Dugan, leadership is supposed to be hard. Not everyone is called to lead. But God has uniquely called and prepared you for your leadership journey.

The canoe trips that I made in my younger years during adverse conditions are the ones I tend to remember today. You will encounter headwinds on your leadership journey. Those headwinds may turn into full-fledged storms.

When those storms rage, remember that even though you may be the captain, God is the one in charge!

CHAPTER 7

THE POWER *of* PARTNERSHIPS

· ·

T wo heads are better than one.

This common phrase is simple and straightforward yet packed with wisdom. There are times in life when one has to go it alone. Some people, and leaders, prefer to operate independently. And certainly some situations call for single points of action.

But there is wisdom, strength, and even power in partnerships. As a leader, you have a choice: you and your organization can walk alone, or you can engage with others on the journey.

The concept of two being better than one is a fundamental part of creation. In Genesis 2:18 we read, "Then the LORD God said, 'It is not good that the man should be alone; I will make him a helper fit for him.'"

Two are better than one. Although the Genesis passage is speaking more directly to the relationship between husband and wife, there is an embedded principle that still applies to other aspects of the Christian life and fellowship—and also to leadership.

King Solomon writes:

> **Two are better than one, because they have a good reward for their toil. For if they fall, one will lift up his fellow. But woe to him who is alone when he falls and has not another to lift him up! Again, if two lie together, they keep warm, but how can one keep warm alone? And though a man might prevail**

against one who is alone, two will withstand him—a threefold cord is not quickly broken. (ECCLESIASTES 4:9–12)

Proverbs 15:22 tells us, "Without counsel plans fail, but with many advisers they succeed."

Jesus put this principle in action when He sent out the twelve apostles in pairs of two: "And He called the twelve and began to send them out two by two, and gave them authority over the unclean spirits" (Mark 6:7).

Jesus again set up partnerships as He sent out the seventy-two: "After this the Lord appointed seventy-two others and sent them on ahead of Him, two by two, into every town and place where He Himself was about to go" (Luke 10:1).

Partnerships are part of creation, extolled by Solomon, and put into practice by Jesus. It is pretty hard to argue against the value of partnerships! So, then, what does this mean for leaders?

For those in the for-profit sector, partnerships allow entities to combine resources, to complement organizational strengths, and to achieve efficiencies that increase returns for the stakeholders. Those returns are measured in financial terms.

> IT IS PRETTY HARD TO ARGUE AGAINST THE VALUE OF PARTNERSHIPS!

In the nonprofit sector, partnerships increase mission effectiveness. We measure a partnership's success by the improved outcomes for those the entities serve.

In either case, leaders harness the power of partnerships to move their organizations forward with greater efficiency or in shorter time frames.

Our job as leaders is to get things done. We would be remiss, then, to ignore opportunities to get more things done more quickly with better results.

Lessons Learned Early

My path through the actuarial profession and the insurance industry provided me with experiences that were not always typical. Although the companies and the departments that I worked in provided traditional group insurance, I was also exposed to nontraditional applications of group insurance.

At one company where I worked, we were looking to form strategic alliances with other companies. My company had certain core competencies and competitive advantages that others wanted to capitalize on. We, in turn, saw complementary capabilities in another firm that we hoped to take advantage of. I was part of the team charged with finding ways to bring the two together in ways that met our business objectives.

We didn't always succeed in pulling off the deal. But when we did, the partnership proved valuable to both parties.

At other times, I was part of a team that pulled together complex group life insurance arrangements to meet certain financial objectives of another company while still achieving our own company's goals. These product solutions were uniquely designed and administered and required a great degree of actuarial creativity to meet the objectives of all parties involved.

These assignments early in my career transformed me and my philosophy of how to get things done in ways that continue to influence my thoughts, actions, and decisions today.

Successful partnerships are created and maintained when both parties not only benefit from the relationship in a significant manner but also contribute to its success in a meaningful way.

The benefits derived from a successful partnership need not be comparable. Nor do the contributions need to be equal. Both parties must give, and both parties must get. Insistence on pure equality can doom the endeavor to failure. A commitment to both parties realizing value is fundamental.

Partnering to Benefit the Church

Eventually, I began to work at an entity within The Lutheran Church—Missouri Synod known as Worker Benefit Plans. Today the name is Concordia Plan Services, or simply Concordia Plans. Back then, Worker Benefit Plans had a business philosophy of doing as much as possible in house. That philosophy was never really decided upon; it was just the default position of the organization. There was not a realization that successful partnerships were within reach.

The organization required similar technology and systems as that of an insurance company, yet it had only a fraction of the customer base over which to spread cost. Likewise, complex processes and procedures were in place, comparable to leading benefit organizations, yet we handled a fraction of the workload that the others did.

This was the perfect opportunity to engage in substantial and meaningful partnerships.

Insurance companies and other benefit organizations had systems and structures in place that Worker

THIS WAS THE PERFECT OPPORTUNITY TO ENGAGE IN SUBSTANTIAL AND MEANINGFUL PARTNERSHIPS.

Benefit Plans could take advantage of. As an aggregator of resources across the church, WBP brought a pool of tens of thousands of potential customers and significant revenue streams associated with their employee benefits.

Both parties would contribute to the new partnership. Both parties would benefit from the relationship. Equality was not the goal. Instead, negotiations focused on improved outcomes and increased value for both sides.

WBP got access to products, services, capacity, innovations, and so much more.

The other company would receive administrative fees to cover their marginal expenditures and offset fixed overhead expenses. Managed care organizations that we partnered with received more members, which improved their negotiations with provider networks. We, in turn, benefited from those negotiations. In addition, we no longer needed to process health claims internally and were able to get rid of a health claims payment system.

Both parties gained. Both parties contributed. The gains and contributions were not equal, but both parties realized value.

Here is a fact that many people find surprising: when you combine all the ministries of the LCMS, you get the scope and magnitude of a Fortune 500 company! Here is what I offer in support of that claim. Within rankings of the largest retirement programs in the United States, the retirement programs of the LCMS are typically found somewhere in the 300s. Around us on the list are very common and well-known corporations.

Now, I admit that this is not a direct comparison. But do not miss the bigger point. Our retirement programs represent an aggregation of resources from thousands of small to midsize ministries. It can serve as a proxy for the total payroll for full-time workers at all our ministries combined. This aggregation is comparable to that of major corporations, unions, and other benefit organizations.

What this meant is that WBP, and now Concordia Plan Services, goes to market with a highly desirable customer base. No insurance company or benefits provider wants to work with a ministry that has only one or two full-time employees. They do, however, want very much to work with all of us when we are walking and working together.

For those within the LCMS, consider this: the greatest value is not found in the partnership between Concordia Plans and an insurance company.

THE PARTNERSHIP WITH THE GREATEST, MOST IMPACTFUL AND MEANINGFUL POTENTIAL IS THE PARTNERSHIP OF OUR MINISTRIES WALKING TOGETHER FOR THE COMMON GOOD!

The partnership with the greatest, most impactful and meaningful potential is the partnership of our ministries walking together for the common good! Herein is meaningful and tangible evidence of how, as a church body, we are in fact better together.

When we go to market as one entity, we command the attention of best-in-class vendors and providers. We have significant leverage in negotiation, which carries on to the management of those relationships. The result is lower expenses for Concordia Plans and for all the participating ministries.

Our risk pools are large enough for us to insure ourselves. By insuring ourselves, we get to set the terms and parameters of the coverages, much like large companies do for their employee base. This results in far more bang for the buck!

Going alone, a ministry may face a scarcity of resources. At times, we can all get caught up in a scarcity mentality. But the reality is that God has richly blessed our church.

Walking together, we see how richly blessed our Synod is!

Results of Our Partnership in Ministry

I know that is a lot of great talk, but can it be backed up with results? Absolutely!

Health insurance, especially in the small-employer market, is largely about payment and reimbursement of health claims. Claims costs are managed by keeping care in network and by restricting coverage.

In the Concordia Health Plan, we partner with carriers to access provider networks and associated discounts and to manage the claims process. But the real value is found in improved outcomes and in successfully helping church workers become healthier.

The results are real and measurable. We are able to measure improvements in the overall health status of our church worker population. Those who engage in health and wellness programs show a lower overall health risk profile. Perhaps the greatest proof is found in the fact that annual cost increases for our health plan have consistently been market rates of increase!

In our church health plan, we are not simply reimbursing claims. We are helping church workers maintain and even improve their health!

If our thousands of ministries looked to obtain retirement programs on their own, the available products would come with significantly higher fees to participants. These increased fees include charges to cover administrative expenses, and there are typically embedded investment management fees as well. These additional fees drag down overall investment performance, meaning a lower level of accumulated value.

BY AGGREGATING OUR RESOURCES, CHURCH WORKERS BENEFIT.

Once again, by aggregating our resources, church workers benefit by realizing larger retirement accounts! Another great benefit of consolidating resources is found in the underlying investment portfolio of our retirement programs. The larger pool of assets under management provides greater opportunities for diversification, which, in turn, enhances return and mitigates risk.

Even more is accomplished when entities of the church come together. Concordia Plans has partnered with The Lutheran Church—Missouri Synod Foundation in the area of investments. When the two organizations have opportunities to utilize a common investment manager, we negotiate fees based on the combined assets from both partners. The investments are not comingled, and the investment committee of each board retains full control over its respective assets. The investment manager simply agrees to a lower fee structure. The result is hundreds of thousands of dollars in savings each year. This is an incredible return on one simple act of collaboration!

Seeing Broader Opportunities to Partner

Concordia Plan Services manages the employee benefit trusts on behalf of The Lutheran Church—Missouri Synod. Other denominations have similar organizations. Many years ago, the leaders of these organizations discovered great value in coming together.

The Church Benefits Association has a membership of around fifty denominational benefit organizations. CBA members collectively manage over $125 billion in net assets and provide employee benefits for over 150,000 ministries. CBA members cover more than 250,000 workers, plus family members.

The first gathering of church benefit organizations took place in 1915, and they have been gathering every year since then.

A primary focus for the CBA has been learning from one another and sharing best practices. We have a distinct advantage over other trade organizations in that we are not in competition with one another. Instead, we are all called to serve the ministries and workers of our respective church bodies. We do not discuss theology and instead focus on the challenges we share in carrying out our mission of support.

The employee benefit world is extremely complex. I do not have a simple way to measure the value we receive from this collaboration. But after attending these meetings for nearly twenty-five years, I can say with confidence that this collaboration with peers has driven significant value to Concordia Plan Services and those we serve!

> THIS COLLABORATION WITH PEERS HAS DRIVEN SIGNIFICANT VALUE TO CONCORDIA PLAN SERVICES AND THOSE WE SERVE!

In 2001, several church plan leaders came together to envision a more tangible way of working together. I was fortunate to be part of a small group that explored the possibility of forming a purchasing coalition. As we saw the value of numbers within our own benefit plans, we began to imagine what greater purchasing power might come if the pool of customers was even larger.

We quickly settled on investigating a purchasing coalition for prescription drugs within our health plans. Already in the early 2000s, we were seeing more complexity and significantly higher costs in this portion of our benefit program.

In 2001, we successfully created and implemented a church plan purchasing coalition for prescription drugs. Our respective plans continued to operate separately, and our boards maintained full control of the plans and plan designs. But we all benefited from a significant decrease in fees and increases in rebates.

In the first year alone, our health plan realized a savings of five million dollars. Over time, that annual savings has grown even larger. Today, the ministries of the LCMS have saved well over one hundred million dollars! Those savings are directly realized by ministries through lower benefit costs, meaning the dollars stay within the local ministry.

Church Plans and Washington, DC

There is another way that leaders of church benefit organizations come together to improve outcomes for those we serve. The top executives of thirty-five denominational benefit programs make up the membership of the Church Alliance.[6]

The benefit programs that we manage are considered church plans under federal law and regulation. It is important that lawmakers and regulators understand the important role our organizations play in the support of our church bodies and our local ministries. Our benefit programs are designed in a way that allows us to care for our own and to do so in ways that align with our respective beliefs.

Much of our work is in the details of retirement plan administration and compliance. Often lawmakers overlook church plans as they consider retirement-related legislation. The Church Alliance works to ensure that valuable legislation extends to church plans, and we work to protect church plans from inappropriate or burdensome regulation.

Very few members of congress are part of The Lutheran Church—Missouri Synod. However, nearly every member of congress identifies with one of the Church Alliance denominations. Some are current and active members of a congregation or synagogue; some grew up in a church or married into one. It is rare to walk into a Senate or House office on behalf of the Church Alliance and not be warmly welcomed.

What one quickly realizes is that the Church Alliance provides lawmakers with a rare and valuable opportunity. Church Alliance

6   To learn more about our collaborative work, see www.church-alliance.org.

members cover the theological and political spectrum, but we only come with issues or concerns that are nonpartisan and without controversy. The Church Alliance allows legislators to focus on policy rather than politics. It gives them opportunities to demonstrate effective leadership and deliver results to those they serve.

I will share a bit more about the work of the Church Alliance in the next chapter. For now, the Church Alliance—with its collaborative work and tangible results—provides another example of the power and value of partnerships.

Hidden Potential

As a leader, it is my responsibility to deliver results on behalf of stakeholders and customers. The same is true for you and all leaders. I am convinced that when partnerships are well thought out and well structured, they can serve as catalysts, or accelerators, of value.

Potential partnerships are not always evident, and so leaders need to seek them out. As you seek out these opportunities, you must have clarity of purpose and of mission so that you can properly assess the potential value of a new relationship. As leader, you must have an honest assessment of your organization's strengths and weaknesses (or perhaps gaps in capability or capacity) so that you can properly assess how another entity can serve as an effective complement to your organization.

> A LEADER MUST BE BOLD IN ENVISIONING A NEW WAY TO DO THINGS.

A leader must be bold in envisioning a new way to do things. And the leader must be proactive and pursue new opportunities.

Within the church body that I serve, I see an abundance of potential partnerships just waiting to be taken advantage of. As our ministries face the challenges of the current economy, and as we face significant demographic headwinds, effective partnerships can drive real change.

Partnerships Right within Reach

Partnerships can begin right at home. It saddens me to see so many ministries divide their organization into the "church side" and the "school side"—two ministry "silos" existing in the same building and serving the same families.

It gives me great joy to be at a congregation that views its ministry in a holistic way. We are a church and a school—both/ and, not either/or. That deliberate mindset makes a big difference in how we operate and in the community that has been created.

It saddens me when I see churches view neighboring congregations as competitors. Church-hoppers certainly help fuel that fire, but it is not an excuse to close in on ourselves.

I encourage us, instead, to envision how communities can be more richly blessed when God's people work together for the sake of the Kingdom!

Our battle is with sin, death, and the power of the devil. It is not with the neighboring congregation to which we lost some members.

Two are better than one! Reach out, connect, collaborate, and cooperate—all for the sake of the community that desperately needs to know the Savior!

> REACH OUT, CONNECT, COLLABORATE, AND COOPERATE—ALL FOR THE SAKE OF THE COMMUNITY THAT DESPERATELY NEEDS TO KNOW THE SAVIOR!

Likewise, imagine how our schools could function more like a system— combining or sharing resources in a way that blesses the work of all.

Over the course of nearly twenty-five years of working within the church, I have attended many meetings and conferences filled with talk of how we could work together for the sake of ministry. After the meetings, however, we all go our separate ways and continue to operate as we always have. I am guilty of doing this myself.

As leaders, we have an obligation to increase stakeholder value (however that is defined or measured in your context). Strategic partnerships have incredible potential to accelerate and multiply results. My encouragement to you as a leader, or as an emerging leader, is to aggressively pursue strategic partnerships.

Do not get caught up in a mentality of scarcity, but instead prayerfully consider the rich resources that God has placed all around. Pray for the wisdom, creativity, and courage to develop partnerships that will move ministry forward in new and exciting ways!

CHAPTER 8

THE POWER
of GRATITUDE

· ·

A s a child is beginning to speak, one of the first lessons parents teach is to say please and thank you. As a grandfather to four, it makes my heart melt to hear their little voices echo the sounds they have been encouraged to say. Who doesn't laugh when the response to "What do you say?" is "Please!" when it was supposed to be "Thank you" or vice versa?

Parents instill these disciplines to help their children develop the habit of saying please and thank you, as children learn early on to mimic the responses. Developing good manners is an important part of children's growth and development and something that they will continue to use into their adult lives.

But when do we develop the capacity to truly *feel* thankful?

Growing up, our sons didn't always get along. Arguments and sometimes even fights would occur. As a part of the reconciliation process, my wife and I would instruct them to tell each other "I'm sorry."

They would always end up saying it. And a few times—very few—they would even mean it. Usually, their posture and tone of voice made it perfectly clear they were only saying it to appease Mom and Dad. My solution would then be to have them say it "like you mean it." It was a brilliant strategy on my part as they would respond with only a slightly better tone of voice. The insincerity continued to hang in the air like a gigantic storm cloud.

Oh, I used my parental authority to get them to say the words. But that authority could not change their hearts.

Teaching someone to *say* thank you is relatively easy.

Teaching someone to *be* thankful is another matter completely.

There are events in life that are so overwhelming that a profound sense of gratitude comes over me. This year, we welcomed two new grandchildren to the fold. As I sit and hold these beautiful gifts from God, my heart overflows with gratitude. God has blessed me in so many ways!

But truth be told, I do not always feel that profound sense of gratitude in the day-in and day-out routines in life.

> TEACHING SOMEONE TO *BE* THANKFUL IS ANOTHER MATTER COMPLETELY.

A Thankful King

Scripture tells us that King David was a man after God's own heart (1 Samuel 13:14; Acts 13:22). It would seem, then, that we could learn much from his character and his behaviors along his leadership journey.

Certainly, David had his faults and his failures. But in the book of Psalms, we see him expressing the hope and confidence he had in his God, his Creator and Redeemer. The Psalms are also filled with expressions of thankfulness.

In my English translation, some form of the word *thank* is used over fifty times in the Psalms. That amount can hardly be considered a casual reference. I remember being taught that when studying the Bible, we should pay special attention to those things that are repeated. Such repetition would more than suggest that a spirit of thanksgiving, of giving thanks to God, should be an important part of the Christian life and walk.

> A SPIRIT OF THANKSGIVING, OF GIVING THANKS TO GOD, SHOULD BE AN IMPORTANT PART OF THE CHRISTIAN LIFE AND WALK.

When I was a child, my family would at times have meals at the homes of great uncles and aunts on my mom's side. We always offered a prayer of thanksgiving before we ate, but when we were at the home of my great uncle John, we would also pray after the meal was completed. Uncle John would lead us in returning thanks. Together we would pray, "Give thanks to the Lord, for He is good, and His mercy endures forever."

When I was young, I gave little thought to the broader lives of my uncles and aunts. But as I got older, I realized that I was blessed to be surrounded by these good and godly men and women. I remember attending the retirement dinner for Uncle John. As I listened to various people speak about him, my eyes began to open a bit. At the time, praying twice was just something we did at Uncle John's house. Today I recognize the spirit of deep and profound gratitude that guided Uncle John. That spirit carried over into his career and his relationships with others.

I later discovered that Uncle John's prayer of thanksgiving comes from Scripture itself. We find it and other prayers of thanksgiving to God all throughout the Psalms, again emphasizing its importance.

If the leader of God's people, the appointed king of Israel, took such a posture of thanksgiving, what should that mean for you and me on our leadership journeys?

A Thankful Leader in the Early Church

Across the letters written by the apostle Paul, the theme of thanksgiving shows up over forty times. Like David, Paul had his share of challenges. And like David, Paul exhibited a spirit of thankfulness.

> LIKE DAVID, PAUL EXHIBITED A SPIRIT OF THANKFULNESS.

Paul's expressions of gratitude differ from those of David, which is to be expected. First, they lived in very different times and served in different ways, and no two people think or speak exactly alike. Second, their writings have different purposes—one is a book of poems and the other a set of letters. But each displays a strong and consistent posture of gratitude to his Creator and Redeemer!

Paul encourages his listeners to follow his example of thankfulness:

> Let your reasonableness be known to everyone. The Lord is at hand; do not be anxious about anything, but in everything by prayer and supplication *with thanksgiving* let your requests be made known to God. And the peace of God, which surpasses all understanding, will guard your hearts and your minds in Christ Jesus. (PHILIPPIANS 4:5–7, EMPHASIS ADDED)

> And above all these put on love, which binds everything together in perfect harmony. And let the peace of Christ rule in your hearts, to which indeed you were called in one body. *And be thankful.* Let the word of Christ dwell in you richly, teaching and admonishing one another in all wisdom, singing psalms and hymns and spiritual songs, with thankfulness in your hearts to God. And whatever you do, in word or deed, do everything in the name of the Lord Jesus, *giving thanks to God the Father* through Him. (COLOSSIANS 3:14–17, EMPHASIS ADDED)

> Rejoice always, pray without ceasing, *give thanks* in all circumstances; for this is the will of God in Christ Jesus for you. (1 THESSALONIANS 5:16–18, EMPHASIS ADDED)

A Lesson in Thankfulness

Just before the world shut down due to the COVID-19 pandemic, I had an impactful lesson on the value of giving thanks. The story involves the Church Alliance, an organization I introduced in the previous chapter. The Church Alliance is a network of thirty-five church benefit plan organizations that advocates for employee benefits—including retirement and health care—for clergy, lay workers, and their families. The Church Alliance works to protect the benefits of religious leaders of a variety of religious traditions in nearly every community across the United States.

Concordia Plan Services, the organization I serve, manages the employee benefit programs of The Lutheran Church—Missouri Synod and is a member of the Church Alliance. I have the privilege of serving as chair of the Steering Committee, which acts as the board of directors for the alliance.

The work of the Church Alliance takes me and my counterparts to Washington, DC, on a regular basis to meet with lawmakers, regulators, and their staff members to discuss the unique challenges facing church benefit plans, as well as the ministries and members we serve.

Church Alliance members operate church plans under federal law. Our work falls under a unique legislative and regulatory umbrella. The plans and programs we offer are uniquely designed and operated to support the ministries and workers of our respective denominations. Our goal in meeting with lawmakers is not to work for special rights or privileges for those we serve, but rather to defend our denominations' rights to operate our benefit plans according to our beliefs, and to ensure that our ministries and members are not put at a disadvantage relative to the broader employee benefit regulatory framework.

At the end of 2019, the Church Alliance realized incredible success as three different items of interest to us were included in a flurry of legislation that was passed and quickly signed into law. We often labor for years on issues that never get resolved. Even when we have support from both Republicans and Democrats and support in both the House and the Senate, our items often fail to make it into any sort of legislation that gets passed and signed into law.

This made the events of late 2019 all the more incredible as we saw our first item attached to the year-end bill, then another, and then another!

It was evident we needed to return to Capitol Hill and thank those members of the House and the Senate who served as champions of our church-plan issues.

Truth be told, at first, I balked at the idea. Why should we go back to Washington, DC, to thank people for doing their jobs? At times, I can be as big a cynic as anyone with respect to things that go on in our nation's capital, but the reality is that there are many good people there trying to do what is right for our country and its people.

> THE REALITY IS THAT THERE ARE MANY GOOD PEOPLE . . . TRYING TO DO WHAT IS RIGHT FOR OUR COUNTRY AND ITS PEOPLE.

I quickly relented, realizing it was the right thing to do. My mother would have been proud of me. But I admit that showing gratitude was not my first instinct.

Fast forward to early March 2020 (you remember what happens in a couple of weeks), and we are back on Capitol Hill. I had the opportunity to visit with several senators, while other Church Alliance colleagues covered the House.

Our champions included both Democrats and Republicans. They represented states that are primarily rural and states that are significantly urban. Those we honored were affiliated with both Christian and Jewish denominations.

Our plan was to present our supporters with a thank-you gift to express our gratitude for their willingness to be a church plan champion. We gave each of them a token of our appreciation in the form of an acrylic award that could be displayed in their office for all to see.

Something unusual happened on this trip: in every Senate office that I went to that day, the senator was there in person to greet our group! We often meet only with key staff members, so this was extraordinary.

They held the award with great care and solemnly read aloud what was printed on it. They shook our hands and sincerely thanked *us*!

One of the things I have learned in meeting with lawmakers is that if the senator wants to do the talking, let the senator do the talking! But this made for a very odd turn of events. We were there to thank the lawmakers, but they spent as much, if not more, time thanking us.

And then it hit me.

The reason they were so appreciative of us being there is that they rarely get thanked.

The cynic in me returns now: every one of those senators realizes the incredible power and notoriety that comes with the office he or she holds. The fame and opportunities will follow those senators long after they leave office. Sure, there is pressure, and they are often in the spotlight in challenging ways, but the rewards more than offset those pressures.

THAT DAY, I SAW THE REAL PERSON BEHIND THE TITLE AND THE OFFICE.

Yet, that day, I saw the real person behind the title and the office.

They were truly honored and humbled to receive our thanks and the accompanying award.

Again, my mother would have been proud of me.

That day, one Bible account played through my mind.

A Thankful Leper

Luke 17 shares the account of ten lepers who approached Jesus with a simple request: "Have mercy on us." The passage does not tell us whether they specifically asked for healing. Perhaps the need was so evident that it went without saying. Jesus responded by healing all ten of them, but only one showed gratitude.

> **On the way to Jerusalem [Jesus] was passing along between Samaria and Galilee. And as He entered a village, He was met by ten lepers, who stood at a distance and lifted up their voices, saying, "Jesus, Master, have mercy on us." When He saw them He said to them, "Go and show yourselves to the priests." And as they went they were cleansed. Then one of**

them, when he saw that he was healed, turned back, praising God with a loud voice; and he fell on his face at Jesus' feet, giving Him thanks. Now he was a Samaritan. Then Jesus answered, "Were not ten cleansed? Where are the nine? Was no one found to return and give praise to God except this foreigner?" And He said to him, "Rise and go your way; your faith has made you well." (LUKE 17:11–19)

I would like to think that, if I were healed from such a terrible disease, I would be overwhelmed with gratitude like the one who returned. But I would probably be like the nine, thinking more about me and how my life was changed. I would have been racing ahead to show myself to the priest so that my earthly life could be restored.

Genuine Gratitude

There is much more to the story of those days in Washington, DC, in early 2020.

I cannot emphasize enough how graciously we were received in those Senate offices. These were not significant photo ops for the senators. Oh, we did end up on some Facebook pages and Twitter feeds, but that was not the motivation for the lawmakers. They were truly honored to meet with us.

One other very important thing happened in each of the offices we visited. Toward the end of each gathering, the senator would ask: "What do you need us to work on next?"

Now, we have all been in situations where conversations are concluded with gracious lines that are not necessarily to be taken literally. Someone may say, "Keep in touch," but they are not creating an open invitation for regular dialogue. All parties know that this is a polite ending to a conversation.

But these senators were serious—they wanted to hear what we needed them to work on next. They wanted us to share those items right then. They were not asking us to send a memo to their staff members; they wanted to hear the specifics!

They sincerely wanted to do more for the Church Alliance and the ministries and members we serve.

That day I learned the real power of gratitude.

Yes, it is polite to say thank you. It is a proper and respectful thing to do.

> **GENUINE GRATITUDE CAN BE TRANSFORMATIVE.**

But genuine gratitude can be transformative.

Our simple act of expressing appreciation for the time and effort committed to our cause brought a response of humility and a determination to do even more.

In no way am I suggesting that gratitude be used as a tool for manipulation, like a toddler who tries to receive more by saying please and thank you. But genuine gratitude—gratitude that comes from the heart—is meaningful and impactful. Such gratitude reflects a spirit of humility. This gratitude builds relationships.

Even More to the Story

As you may have gathered, the timing of this story matters. The legislative victories took place at the end of 2019 and our trip to Washington, DC, took place in the first few days of March 2020.

For several weeks, we had been hearing of a dangerous new virus spreading in China. There were accounts of people getting sick and dying from it, and it seemed to spread quickly and easily.

In late February, I began to see people wearing masks on airplanes. During our trip to Washington, DC, something happened that I had not encountered before: many people avoided shaking hands and instead offered "elbow bumps."

Less than two weeks later, the United States was beginning to shut down. Businesses and schools were telling people to stay home. Our organization began a sprint toward remote work. We had no idea whether the congregations and schools we served would be able to pay their bills for employee benefits. The future felt very uncertain.

Congress was observing all of this and contemplating action to keep the economy afloat. One idea that surfaced was to provide relief to the employers that continued to employ and pay workers during the pandemic.

Then came the phone calls. One in particular came from Senator James Lankford of Oklahoma—one of the senators whom I met with personally only days before. The question was simple: What do you and your members need?

God had led Church Alliance leaders to meet with legislators in early March. That visit placed the Church Alliance toward the front of their minds. Their willingness to do more for the church community carried into those early days of the pandemic.

Our response was equally simple: include nonprofit and religious organizations in the COVID relief spending directed toward employers. The goal of those funds was to preserve paychecks, and our ministries and workers also needed their paychecks preserved!

It took no further prompting for our church plan champions to spring into action on our behalf. The Paycheck Protection Program was made available to the churches and schools that we serve!

I have no idea of the economic impact that the PPP had on our ministries overall, but I have heard many accounts of how those funds kept ministries afloat during the pandemic. The funds ensured a cash flow to ministries that might otherwise have been forced to close.

It is incredibly humbling to know that God used the Church Alliance in the remarkable way He did in 2020. As is often the case, we cannot always see God at work in the present moment. But we often can see His hand as we look back.

At the end of 2019, I was on a path of acting like one of the nine healed lepers. But God placed people around me who encouraged me to gather Church Alliance leaders and return to Washington, DC, to express our gratitude to lawmakers for, yes, doing their job.

> GOD, IN HIS INFINITE WISDOM, TURNED THAT SINGLE ACT OF APPRECIATION INTO A WEALTH OF BLESSINGS FOR HIS PEOPLE.

God, in His infinite wisdom, turned that single act of appreciation into a wealth of blessings for His people.

CHAPTER 9

BALANCING OFFENSE
and DEFENSE

. . . .

When my boys were young, I got involved in coaching. I had always been active in athletics, and I have seen how sports can be a positive influence on young people. Unfortunately, I have also seen the negative side of athletic competition. A main motivation for my serving as coach was to ensure a positive experience for my sons and their teammates.

Other dads stepped in for basketball and baseball, and I was happy to be an assistant coach during those seasons. Soccer was the sport for which I primarily served as a head coach.

Unlike most of the other dads, I did play quite a bit of soccer growing up. As a youth, I played for school and rec teams and even played club soccer as that was becoming a thing in Minnesota in the late 1970s. Those experiences allowed me to play one year of soccer while in college.

Growing up, most of our coaches had not played the game themselves. Soccer tended to draw hockey players and coaches who were looking for a sport to participate in during their off-season. The free-flowing play of the two sports created a natural synergy in playing styles and strategies. Our strategies, however, were not well developed.

Developing a Coaching Philosophy

During my early years of coaching, I had the opportunity to complete two levels of training through the National Soccer

Coaches Association of America. Having completed an undergraduate degree in education, I was immediately won over by the focus on child and adolescent development that permeated the coaching curriculum. I wish such training were mandatory for all youth coaches!

The instructor coached the men's and women's soccer teams at a local university. His coaching pedigree was solid. His love of the game was infectious. His passion for instilling a love of the game was inspirational. He outlined fundamental strategies of play that I had never considered before, even though I had spent many hours on the field as a player. My own coaching philosophy began to emerge.

He and I had many great conversations about the beautiful game. I loved the theory behind the instruction but sometimes wrestled with how to apply it to a bunch of seven-year-old boys!

During my years of coaching, I tried to read and absorb as much as I could on coaching and coaching philosophies, on training and systems of play. By the time my sons hit middle school, I had developed a philosophy and system of play that resulted in success for our teams.

Of the many coaching philosophies I was exposed to, there was one I really struggled with. The concept did not seem quite right to me, even contrary to the successful style I had been developing. After long and deep consideration, I ultimately rejected that concept and continued to refine my own approach to play.

The philosophy I struggled with was this: coaches must emphasize either offense or defense, not both. If you try to coach both, you will only end up confusing your players.

As a coach, and thinking back to my time as a player, I could not accept that premise. For the teams I coached, our offense began with our defense. And our defense began with our offense.

Our goal as a team was to win the ball back as quickly as possible whenever we lost possession. My rationale for this is simple: the game is much easier when played in the other team's half. By applying immediate pressure, we could win the ball back more quickly and transition to the attack before the opposing team could move into our half of the field and get reorganized defensively.

It was a system of high pressure whereby aggressive defending led to more goal-scoring opportunities. Offense and defense were intimately and integrally connected. It was not one or the other.

> **OFFENSE AND DEFENSE WERE INTIMATELY AND INTEGRALLY CONNECTED.**

As a season ticket holder for St. Louis City Soccer Club, I greatly enjoy watching a much more advanced and sophisticated version of this style of play being implemented by the new team.

Natural Tendencies

Truth be told, if I am going to lean one way between offense and defense, I would lean toward defense. After all, if you are bad at defense, you'd better be really good on offense because you are going to have to score a lot of goals! But leaning toward defense does not lessen my focus on the attack. Leaning toward defense changes the nature of the attack but not the importance of it.

One aspect of my both/and philosophy tended to get lost at the youth levels: the whole team is responsible for executing our strategy. My players needed to understand that when our team had the ball, everyone was on offense. And when the other team had the ball, everyone was defending. Some coaches and players wanted only the forwards to attack and only the defenders to defend. But soccer doesn't work that way. We attack as a team, and we defend as a team. Defenders score and forwards defend.

After years of playing and coaching multiple sports, I do believe players have natural tendencies toward either defense or offense. I have also concluded that those tendencies carry over into other aspects of life as well.

As I shared above, I tend to lean toward defense, not just as a coach but also as an athlete. In hindsight, my emphasis on defense was most likely due to my lack of offensive abilities. In baseball, I was a lousy hitter, but I was a pretty solid fielder. In basketball, I could not shoot or dribble very well. But again, I was pretty good at defense. On the soccer field, it was much the same.

Most players have a natural tendency toward either offense or defense. It is rare to see a player have a heart and passion for both. I am not talking about the ability to do both—there are players who excel both offensively and defensively. I am talking about their inner drive, their passion, their primary focus.

My middle son was a great example of this. Primarily a midfielder, he could be put up front as a forward or placed in the back with the defenders. His heart, though, always had him drifting back and behind the ball. He was continually protecting the backs of his forwards and giving them support from behind. And he was always dropping back to support his defenders. Unlike his father, he was proficient in both aspects of the game, but he certainly had his natural tendencies.

TOO MUCH OF ONE OR THE OTHER CAN BE A PROBLEM FOR THE LEADER, FOR THE TEAM, AND FOR THE ORGANIZATION.

I believe that leaders also have a natural tendency toward offense or defense. I also believe that our natural tendencies can be highly correlated with our personality. Neither style is right or wrong. But too much of one or the other can be a problem for the leader, for the team, and for the organization.

The Balanced Leader

In soccer, defense and offense must be balanced. They must work together because possession changes often and quickly, and the team must likewise transition efficiently and effectively.

Successful players, teams, and coaches learn and live that balance. One may be favored or emphasized over the other. But successful teams find that balance and synergy where offense and defense work together in harmony.

Football and baseball, by design, have well-defined separation between offense and defense. Soccer and hockey, on the other hand, exhibit a constant state of fluidity between these two aspects of the game.

That constant state of fluidity is true for leadership as well.

As leaders, we must find and live in that balance between offense and defense. Too much or too little of either can drive an organization to ruin.

Consider an overly strong emphasis on offense. In this situation, business growth may be so strongly emphasized that poor decisions are made in order to achieve that growth. Perhaps prices are cut so much that new customers are not profitable even when the sale is made. The financial impact of these decisions is typically not felt immediately, and the organization lives for a while on the high of growth, like a rush of sugar. That success might lead to even more aggressive pricing concessions. Eventually, these pricing decisions catch up with an organization, crashing as the sugar high wears off.

Or perhaps quality is sacrificed in order to meet a price point. Once again, the impact may not be felt immediately. But eventually the company's reputation takes a hit. Such reputational damage may take years to reverse—if it can be reversed at all.

Offense is essential for winning the game. The problem comes when there is too much emphasis on growth. In soccer, if a team gets pushed too far up on the attack, it can leave gaping holes for the opponent to exploit on a counterattack.

On the other hand, consider what happens when a leader or organization pays too much attention to defense. In these situations, organizations hunker down and work to preserve or defend what they have. Such approaches can lead a company to ignore market and customer realities. Retaining 100 percent of existing customers is nearly impossible. Without meaningful growth, a slow downward progression ensues. In time, the financial realities set in.

Too much defense, like too much offense, eventually leads to significant and possibly insurmountable challenges.

Leaders must establish that proper balance between offense and defense. We constantly float between the two, applying each as necessary. Like driving a car, the leader must skillfully work the gas pedal and the brake. Both are essential for a safe journey. The art comes in the application. The leader must sense when to apply the brake and when to hit the gas and how much pressure to use. Emergencies usually necessitate hard braking, but otherwise there is no exact science for when and how to apply the brakes or the accelerator. The leader, much like a young driver, must learn through experience.

So, which way do you lean? Do you tend toward the defensive side of leadership? Or do you gravitate toward the offensive side? Great leaders are found in both camps. Neither is right or wrong—the key is balance.

SO, WHICH WAY DO YOU LEAN?

The Defensive Leader

As a leader, you are called to defend your organization. No matter where or how you serve, your organization faces significant risk. You and your team must continually identify and monitor those risks, and you must develop plans to mitigate those risks.

Here are some of the risks my organization faces:

- **Economic**
- **Demographic**
- **Legal and regulatory**
- **Cyber security**
- **Reputational**
- **Competitive**

Your list will, of course, be different, but perhaps you see some similarities. Some types of risk, such as reputational risk, affect virtually all organizations. Not only does the form of risk vary by organization, but the potential magnitude of those risks varies as well.

We need to keep in mind that, as leaders, we are stewards of our respective organizations. Even if we own the business, as Christian leaders, we know that all we have has been given to us by our Creator. We serve as guardians of the resources entrusted to our care. Leaders must have a defensive mindset.

No coach goes into a game without having considered how the opponent will likely formulate a counterattack. Likewise, leaders must be looking and thinking ahead, anticipating and preparing for contingencies. Leaders must think critically and must thoroughly evaluate opportunities and risks. Before making decisions, leaders must understand both the potential rewards and the potential issues that may emerge.

PLOT A COURSE THAT STAYS WELL AWAY FROM POTENTIAL HARM.

One important way to protect your organization from some risks is to plot a course that stays well away from potential harm. For example, you could take your company down a path that goes right up to the legal or regulatory boundary. Or you could chart a similar trajectory that stays a good and safe distance from that line. In both cases, you will have kept your organization in "safe" territory. But one situation leaves no margin for error. Not only that, but it also risks sending a dangerous message to your team about attitudes toward compliance.

Too great an emphasis on defense, however, creates significant problems. Taken too far, risk aversion will paralyze leaders and organizations.

The Offensive Leader

Leaders must recognize that they alone are responsible and accountable for moving their organization forward. With clarity of mission, leaders press their organization forward. New strategies and tactics should be contemplated and implemented. New opportunities must be pursued.

The defensive side works to preserve and retain customers. The offensive side drives toward growth.

Growth does not only mean adding more customers or selling more products to existing customers. Growth can also come in the form of delivering more value to those served. It can come in the form of identifying the emerging needs and wants of customers, and then designing and delivering solutions.

The offensive leader takes calculated risks and moves forward while others hesitate. Once again, such decisions demand that the leader think critically. The situation must be evaluated fully, with risks

> **THE OFFENSIVE LEADER TAKES CALCULATED RISKS AND MOVES FORWARD WHILE OTHERS HESITATE.**

appropriately identified. The offensive leader does not allow analysis paralysis to set in. Instead, after careful deliberation, the leader sets a course of action.

How the Balance Plays Out

My organization manages the employee benefit programs of The Lutheran Church—Missouri Synod. Collectively, we oversee $5 billion of assets that back up the liabilities of the benefit plans.

Those assets are actively invested, meaning that there is exposure to the market and related risk. However, these risks are taken in pursuit of reward. Actuaries are often seen as a risk-averse group. I see it as the exact opposite. Actuaries are trained in evaluating and measuring risk. Having fully considered the risks involved, the assets of the employee benefit plans are invested in order to achieve returns. This allows contributions, or premiums, to be lower as the assets become productive. The investment portfolio is well diversified to capture a wider range of market opportunities but also to act as a mechanism to mitigate risk.

Insurance companies are in the business of taking on risk. In fact, that is the primary product they offer. Insurance premiums are priced in a way that the company profits from taking risk. As Concordia Plans manages the health, life, and disability benefits on behalf of the church, the qualified employee benefit trusts of the LCMS take on the morbidity and mortality risks associated with the benefit programs—ministries and workers insure one another! In doing so, we avoid many costs associated with having those plans fully insured.

Individually, our ministries are not large enough to take on these risks on their own. But by banding together, we achieve a critical mass to realize market efficiencies and achieve targeted outcomes.

These activities, by their very nature, entail a significant assumption of risk. As an offensive leader, I need to lean into that risk and seek what opportunities the market provides. But as a defensive leader, I need to ensure that I take on only prudent risks and employ appropriate risk-mitigation techniques. Offense and defense must be balanced.

OFFENSE AND DEFENSE MUST BE BALANCED.

The book of Matthew contains a parable of three servants, each given an amount of their master's money to invest (Matthew 25:14–19). Two of them found ways to double the master's investment. Presumably, they took on some sort of risk to bring forward such an incredible return. They went on offense. The third, however, hid the money away. Knowing what he did about the master, he became paralyzed with fear. In returning only the master's principal, he in fact robbed the master of even the most basic return on the investment. Offense and defense were not balanced.

Lean toward Defense

It is often said that defense wins championships. In sports, I believe that to be largely true. There are examples to the contrary, but more often than not, defense makes the difference. For those who follow the National Hockey League and the annual run for the Stanley Cup, how often do deep playoff runs depend on a hot goaltender? Look at the St. Louis Blues in 2019. In January, they were at the bottom of the league and brought in a goalie who was fourth on the depth chart at the start of the season. The season ended with the team hoisting the Stanley Cup.

It is ingrained into my personality: defense first. Prevent the other team from scoring and then pursue opportunities to attack.

In my role today, leadership involves risk identification and mitigation first. Retain. Protect. Defend.

I encourage leaders to lean toward defense first, even if your natural inclination is toward offense. Perhaps this is because of my personal bias, but as I stated above, if you are not solid on defense, you had better be really strong on offense!

But it cannot stop there for me or my organization—or for you and yours. As leaders, we must ensure we make progress toward fulfilling our mission. And this involves identifying new ways to serve our stakeholders. Maintaining the status quo is not an option.

Every leader, myself included, must continually keep afoot on the gas. The leader is called to push the organization ever forward. Progress must be ensured.

MAINTAINING THE STATUS QUO IS NOT AN OPTION.

There are appropriate times to accelerate. And there are appropriate times to decelerate. But keep in mind that even as a driver slows down, the vehicle is still moving forward!

Leaders must live, and even thrive, in the balance of offense and defense. This aspect of leadership is far more art than science. And for me it is one of the most compelling and rewarding parts of my leadership journey!

CHAPTER 10

IT'S ALL ABOUT
the PEOPLE

. . . .

E arly in my career, I attended a conference in New York City. As is the case with these types of events, there was a prominent keynote speaker. Unfortunately, I do not remember who the speaker was.

I also do not remember exactly when this event took place, but I do recall that it was prior to me becoming CEO of my organization. That would mean that I was in a senior role and reporting to the then-current president. It also means that I was in my late thirties or early forties.

Now I do remember the location—the famed Waldorf Astoria Hotel. At that point in my career, I had not traveled as extensively as I have today. New York City was a bit overwhelming to this native Midwesterner. To this day, I enjoy my visits to the Big Apple, but to be honest I want to get in, do my business, and get out!

But that day in New York City, as I listened to the keynote speaker, I was more of a critic than a fan.

A couple of reasons for that skepticism are obvious to me today. First of all, I had nowhere near enough experience to understand the wisdom of what I was hearing. There is really nothing I could do about that. In time, I would live and work through experiences that proved true the points the speaker was making.

The second reason for the skepticism is a little embarrassing today.

The Speech

One thing (of many) that I did not understand at the time was that speakers often use these keynote speeches to showcase material from an upcoming book of theirs. As I recall, this particular book was not yet available, and no doubt the speech increased awareness that likely resulted in future sales.

I remember taking notes during the speech, but I have no idea where those notes have ended up. The speech centered around ten or twelve key points, most of which I agreed with or accepted after hearing the explanation. Once again, I do not remember what those points were.

But two specific points I remember very well. I remember them so well because I disagreed with them. Today, however, I am absolutely convinced that the two points are correct and that leaders would be wise to embrace them!

The first point was one that I more shrugged off than rejected outright. The speaker's encouragement was to get more youth involved in your organization. In hindsight, I believe this idea did not resonate with me because I was too young. I may even have been in the category of young people he was talking about.

At that point in time, I was fairly young in comparison to my peers inside the organization and across similar organizations. I did not have the breadth of experience that I have today, which kept me from being able to appreciate the wisdom the speaker shared. Now that I am in my sixties, with less hair—a large percentage of it being gray—I understand fully what the speaker was saying that day.

I have witnessed plenty of examples of emerging leaders delivering incredible value to their organization when given a chance. Many young leaders have a passion and energy that is exciting to watch play out.

GET MORE YOUNG PEOPLE INVOLVED! BUT BE THERE TO COACH AND TO MENTOR THEM.

Their spirit can be infectious and motivate all of us old timers to up our game!

Get more young people involved! But be there to coach and to mentor them. Be there to help them avoid the big mistakes and be there to help build them back up when mistakes are made.

Investment in emerging leaders pays dividends both now and into the future.

It's All about the People

The second, and much larger, point that I remember disagreeing with went something like this: It is all about the people.

Here is where my embarrassment today comes in—from the narrowmindedness or perhaps even arrogance that kept me from learning from this expert.

I heard what was being said, and I fully understood it. I just didn't buy into it. Sure, people are important, but to me there was so much more to it all.

Here I was, a Fellow of the Society of Actuaries and a Member of the American Academy of Actuaries. I had worked in prominent insurance companies—maybe not household names, but certainly recognized leaders in their areas of specialty.

At that time, I was a vice president of a complex financial services organization that was part of one of the largest denominations in the country.

The speaker simply did not understand the complexity of the type of work I was in or of the organization I was serving. Certainly, the people are important. But other things were, in my opinion at the time, much more important.

Actuarial valuations, stochastic forecasting, asset/liability modeling, pricing schematics, reserve calculations, financial projections, vendor manager and performance, long-term financial solvency, technology infrastructure, regulation and compliance, asset allocation—all this and more was what would make or break our business model.

My apologies to that keynote speaker, but he just didn't get it. My world was too complex for his simple solution.

Years later, I landed in the top role in my organization. I have served as president and CEO for over fifteen years. I am still an actuary (although they don't let me near the numbers anymore), and I still have deep expertise in the management of employee benefit programs. I can still navigate the complexities of the business, financial and operational. I can still challenge our outside consultants.

And with all of this knowledge and experience, I can say with 100 percent certainty that the speaker that day was correct: *It is all about the people!*

The People

One of a leader's most important responsibilities is to recruit, develop, and retain a high-performing team. As leader, you cast a vision and ensure alignment, and then you let them do their thing.

It is your responsibility to define expectations and then to hold people accountable for meeting them. You must provide clarity at the front end, and you must be fair and consistent in reviewing performance at the back end.

Get the right people on board, get them aligned, and get out of the way!

The success of your organization depends on your people.

The success of your people depends on you.

> GET THE RIGHT PEOPLE ON BOARD, GET THEM ALIGNED, AND GET OUT OF THE WAY!

Let's return to athletics for a moment. Great players, in many ways, do not need a coach. Great teams, however, need great coaches. Great coaches get the best out of every player and can get players to perform at new and higher levels. Great coaches get great players to work together as a unit in order to achieve more.

Great coaches know that it is all about the players. They know that it is their job to prepare the team and then get out of the way and let them do their thing.

Recruitment

The leader sets the tone with respect to recruiting. Are you looking to simply fill chairs, or are you actively working to find the right people to join in your mission?

Too often organizations will simply settle for someone, especially in a tough labor market, rather than work to find the right candidate. Or perhaps if salaries cannot be competitive with what the market may offer, it can be tempting to take whatever you can get.

Sometimes certain red flags with candidates are overlooked or downplayed—perhaps in the hope that those challenging behaviors or tendencies can be worked through or worked around. In very rare situations, that may be possible. But more often than not, these people become a cancer in the organization and bring more harm than good to the team.

As the accountable leader in your organization, you must set the standard, beginning with your direct reports. Insistence on maintaining high standards begins with you. If you do not bring in high-quality leaders, do not expect others in the organization to follow.

> IT IS ALL ABOUT THE PEOPLE. AND IT BEGINS WITH THE PEOPLE YOU BRING INTO THE ORGANIZATION.

As the speaker observed, it is all about the people. And it begins with the people you bring into the organization.

Development

The right people want to contribute to the organization. They want to add value. They want to grow and develop as individuals and as professionals.

Growth and development is not limited to an upward trajectory on the org chart. Many people are content with the roles and responsibilities they have; they enjoy and find value in their service. They are not looking to move up the corporate ladder. But they do want to learn and to contribute.

> **GROWTH AND DEVELOPMENT IS NOT LIMITED TO AN UPWARD TRAJECTORY ON THE ORG CHART.**

Once you have the right people in the organization, as leader, you must ensure that they are getting the appropriate training and development opportunities. Your people must be coached and mentored for success. Your people must have the appropriate resources and training to further the mission of the organization.

Growth and professional development must be the norm, otherwise stagnation or decline sets in.

As the speaker observed, it is all about the people. And leaders must instill a culture of learning and growth.

Retention

Leaders at all levels of the organization must be dedicated to growing and developing talent, especially when it comes to emerging leaders.

In small organizations, and especially in nonprofit entities, there may not be enough opportunities for up-and-coming leaders to engage and thrive. This is an organizational risk and often a reality.

> **GIVING NEW CHALLENGES AND OPPORTUNITIES TO THESE INDIVIDUALS BUILDS A SENSE OF TRUST AND COMMITMENT.**

Senior leaders can play a critical role, however, in retaining top talent. One simple but meaningful step is to express appreciation. The knowledge that a senior leader sees and values an individual's work can go a long way to instill a sense of belonging and purpose in that person.

Giving new challenges and opportunities to individuals builds a sense of trust and commitment.

In my time as CEO, we have brought many younger leaders into meetings with our board committees. They have opportunities to present their work to the board and to put forward recommendations. Although there is an element of risk for the CEO and senior leaders, the risk is worth the investment in the people.

As the speaker observed, it is all about the people. And senior leaders are accountable for recruiting, developing, and retaining talent.

The Culture

As the accountable executive, you are responsible for your organization's culture. Each of the previous three sections—recruitment, development, and retention—are elements of the culture that you establish.

CULTURES ARE CREATED THROUGH MODELING BEHAVIORS.

Every organization has a culture. Even if you have not been intentional about creating it, the culture exists nonetheless.

Cultures are not, and cannot be, created by mandating behaviors. Cultures are created through modeling behaviors.

Imagine your organization is a neighborhood. What makes for a great neighborhood?

I have lived in neighborhoods with a homeowner association, with indentures or covenants, and those things do not make for great neighborhoods. Although they may seem official and potentially binding, indentures typically lack any real teeth. Violations are turned over to the HOA trustees, who then approach (or don't) the violator. Some violators are simply unaware and therefore change their behavior to align with the neighborhood. But many times, violators are unwilling to change, and neighborhood conflict emerges.

Ultimately, what makes for a great neighborhood is a collection of neighbors choosing to be neighborly.

The quality of the neighborhood is not determined by the HOA or the covenants. The quality of the neighborhood is determined by the residents.

And so it is with corporate culture. Missions, visions, and values establish the norms and expectations. The people decide to live it out—or not.

Unlike in neighborhoods, it is possible to punish or even fire those who choose not to comply in an employment situation. But this is the worst possible way to develop and grow the culture.

Lutheran Christians know that the Law cannot change hearts. Such change comes only through the Gospel. Likewise, workplace "law" cannot change hearts.

Instead, the desired culture must be modeled by leaders, and it starts at the top! From there, it must cascade through the entire organization.

As the speaker observed, it is all about the people. And it is the leader's job to establish a culture where people can grow and thrive!

Engagement

One way to evaluate an organization's culture is to assess engagement. Engaged workers are a sign of a healthy, vibrant culture. Engaged workers are also more productive and deliver higher levels of service.

> ENGAGED WORKERS ARE A SIGN OF A HEALTHY, VIBRANT CULTURE.

Our organization enjoys high satisfaction scores as well as high net promotor scores from those we serve. We also demonstrate high levels of employee engagement based on surveys of our workers. Our scores in all areas far exceed the norms of comparable industries.

I do not believe that it is coincidental that our outside scores and our inside scores are both stellar. In fact, I believe they are highly correlated.

In our organization, we take our employee engagement surveys very seriously. Not only do we look at the numerical scores, but we also pore through the written responses. The assessments are voluntary, and we achieve very high participation levels. They are also anonymous, resulting in candid feedback.

We implement solution teams to review the results and to help us address any deficiencies. We report the results back to our teams, and we also report our intended courses of action.

> THIS IS HOW WE DEMONSTRATE OUR COMMITMENT TO IMPROVEMENTS.

The process is open and transparent. This is how we demonstrate our commitment to improvements.

The results are incredible! For the past three years, our organization has been named a top workplace in St. Louis, Missouri, and was recently named to a list of top workplaces in the nation.

I could not be prouder of our team and the culture we have created together!

And the blessings continue with respect to acquiring talent. As I write this book, there is a broader war for talent raging in our country. Quality and qualified talent is in demand. Even nonprofits are feeling the impact. As a nonprofit, we will never be able to compete based on compensation alone. But a fair compensation structure, coupled with a strong culture and a compelling mission, has allowed us to attract some incredible individuals to our team.

As the speaker observed, it is all about the people!

Taking Care of Your People

Perhaps the biggest heartaches in my career have come in seeing how often we within the church fail to care for the people we call or hire into ministry. Hang around for a while, and you will hear stories of ministries "balancing the budget on the backs of church workers."

Too often, I hear lay leaders say, "That's not how we do it where I work." Of course, they are forgetting the fact that their places of work offer financial rewards for those with master's and doctoral degrees.

In our church, we require students to take on a large cost of education in order to be ordained or commissioned ministers of religion, and then we reward them with below-market salaries. Then we wonder why church workers are so far in debt or why teachers leave Lutheran schools after five years.

As the speaker observed, it is all about the people.

Many years ago, the corporate sector understood that they were in a competition for talent. Today the war for talent is putting even more pressure on businesses. Providing market-based compensation is a reality for employers. To put it another way, market-based salaries are just the first step in attracting and retaining talent.

In the church, we do not want people who are only looking at salary. But at the same time, as leaders, we need to ensure that our workers are provided reasonable wages. The church should not take advantage of the worker's sense of calling. Yet so often I hear of church work families who must cover their dependents under governmental health programs because the ministry fails to provide coverage. Even more appalling is the fact that the household wages are so low that the family is eligible for subsidized care.

> AS LEADERS, WE NEED TO ENSURE THAT OUR WORKERS ARE PROVIDED REASONABLE WAGES.

As you know, I am an actuary, not a theologian. But I believe Scripture speaks in clear and compelling language about compensation:

For the laborer deserves his wages. (LUKE 10:7)

For the Scripture says, "You shall not muzzle an ox when it treads out the grain," and, The laborer deserves his wages. (1 TIMOTHY 5:18)

For the laborer deserves his food. (MATTHEW 10:10)

These passages speak in different ways depending on your role in the situation. When Jesus sent out laborers, as in the Luke and Matthew passages above, they were not to take anything with them on the ministry journey and instead were to depend on the people they ministered to for their wages. Likewise, church workers today are called to rely on God's provision.

The implication for lay leaders in the church is much different. We are to provide for the needs of those who have been called to serve us. Out of Christian care and concern, we make sure that our church workers and their families are taken care of.

Compensation is more than just salary. In the United States, a social contract exists between employers and employees. Our employment system makes comprehensive benefits an integral part of the overall compensation package.

All of this is expensive. But making church workers and their families bear the brunt of the financial burden is no solution.

Let's come at this from another direction. The paragraphs above were a bit heavy on the law, but there is another way to think about taking care of people.

Imagine a setting where a ministry organization commits to providing fair compensation. The ministry puts the marker in the ground, declaring its desire to make sure that the church worker family is taken care of. In this setting, all church workers are taken care of, not just the senior pastor.

In this scenario, compensation is fair, relative to the cost of living, church-body guidelines, and other available benchmarks. And the compensation package includes a comprehensive employee-benefits package.

In our economy, full-time workers enjoy comprehensive health care coverage as part of their benefits package. The corporate world long ago moved beyond simply reimbursing health care expenses into providing robust health and wellness programs. The reason is twofold: first, there is a real and measurable impact on the cost of health care as total cost and the trend in cost are reduced. And second, workers are healthier and therefore more engaged and resilient in their work.

By providing fair compensation and robust health benefits, the ministry will then benefit from healthier workers. Good health does not guarantee results for the ministry. But poor health certainly puts strain on the worker and has a negative impact on ministry.

Providing a retirement program is another way of caring for church workers. In the secular world, workers have access to such programs. Many workers benefit from profit-sharing arrangements or have opportunity to purchase company stock. Business owners and farmers build equity. Ministers of religion pay the entire cost of Social Security through self-employment tax. Providing comprehensive retirement programs, including retirement savings programs, is another way of ensuring workers are cared for now and into retirement.

Beyond a Bias

No doubt I can be accused of a bit of bias regarding this topic, given what my organization does on behalf of the ministries and the workers of the church. But for nearly twenty-five years, I have seen firsthand the blessings that God pours out onto His workers through our collective work! As CEO, I am often the recipient of the thanks and appreciation from workers who have been cared for by the church.

It is overwhelming to hear the accounts! Over and over again, people offer to share their individual stories with others. They know that the cost of coverage is not insignificant for ministries to

THESE STORIES ARE WHY I DO WHAT I DO AND WHY I FEEL SO BLESSED TO BE USED BY GOD IN THIS WAY.

bear, so they want people to know the impact these programs have had on their lives. These stories are why I do what I do and why I feel so blessed to be used by God in this way.

It Is All about the People

At the time, I was not open to the wisdom that the speaker was sharing with his audience at the Waldorf Astoria Hotel in New York. Today, I am older and wiser, and I pray a bit more humbly.

Technical skills and knowledge are critical for success. Strategic plans must be developed and implemented. Creativity and innovation are needed to move organizations forward. Revenue generation is essential. Industry and market experience must be brought to the table. Financial models and projections are needed. Goals and objectives must be established.

All of this is important. All of this is necessary.

But leaders must understand and embrace this central principle if they want to be successful over the long term: it is all about the people!

CHAPTER 11

LEADING
with VALUES

Mission and vision statements are mainstays of organizational strategies. Despite their ubiquitous nature, they are not uniformly understood or applied. There are different schools of thought with respect to what missions or visions should entail. For example, are mission or vision statements intended to be achievable, or are they aspirational? Are they measurable, or are they unquantifiable? Are they finite, or do they live on into perpetuity?

Even knowledgeable experts do not agree on the answers to these questions, and compelling arguments can be made on either side of the debate. To be honest, I do not have strong feelings one way or another. I am not sure it really matters where one ends up on these questions, but two things do matter.

First, do the mission and vision statements provide clarity of purpose and direction? Do they inform and guide decisions about which activities to pursue versus which should be set aside? Can they be used to prioritize initiatives so that the best and most impactful ideas move forward? Do they serve as guideposts to assess progress?

Second, and perhaps more important, are the mission and vision statements actually put to use?

Definitions vary, but what matters is that the mission and vision statements are appropriately applied and used.

The Value of Values

As important as mission and vision statements are in clarifying strategic direction, I believe that values are what ultimately make the biggest impact on the success, or lack thereof, of an organization.

Missions and visions can tell you why an organization exists, what it does, and what it is trying to achieve. Values tell a much more intimate story—they describe who you are!

VALUES TELL A MUCH MORE INTIMATE STORY—THEY DESCRIBE WHO YOU ARE!

Because of this, values are intrinsically internal. Values serve as a moral compass for the organization.

Missions and visions can attract a variety of individuals to an organization. These statements can be exciting and motivating. But an individual's success and ability to effectively contribute to the work of the organization over the long term depends on his or her level of alignment with the organizational values.

Values form the fabric of an organization's culture. Team members who do not believe in or adhere to the values of the entity are ultimately going to clash with the culture.

Organizational Values

Whether or not they have been defined and articulated, your organization has a set of values. These values are embedded in the norms of your culture. They play out regularly as your team carries out their work together and when they interact with one another, in every conversation and meeting. Organizational values are also a part of every interaction with external parties, including your customers and stakeholders.

Unfortunately, leaders cannot simply define the values of the organization and broadcast them to the team for implementation. That strategy is about as effective as when I would tell one of my sons to be nice to his brother. It might work for a moment—at least while Dad is still in the room. My admonition to be nice might impact the immediate, outward behaviors, but my efforts fell way short of changing hearts.

A coach, mentor, and friend of mine would often say, "You hire people for what they know and you fire them for who they are."

The "who they are" is often revealed when a person's behaviors conflict with the values of the organization. I am not talking about a one-time incident when a person had a lapse of judgement or perhaps let personal anger or frustration get the best of him or her. The misalignment of values emerges over a period of time, and often a subtle pattern of behavior is established.

There can be serious consequences if that pattern is not addressed when it first becomes evident. It is said that leadership supports that which it condones. If that is true, then leaders are obligated to take action when observed behaviors collide with the organization's values.

In an ideal world, these sorts of things would be addressed as part of the recruitment process. But hiring for values is a challenge. There is an initial focus on the skills and experiences of a candidate, usually neatly described in the persons's résumé. The degree of fit is relatively easy to assess at this point. Even if the résumé is not a perfect match for the position, you can often get a sense of whether the person can be trained and developed to fill in around those gaps.

HIRING FOR VALUES IS A CHALLENGE.

Well-prepared candidates have researched your organization before coming into an interview. They may have an understanding of the mission of the organization and be prepared to share how their résumé aligns with and supports the organization's mission. But how does one really probe for alignment of values?

Myriad assessment tools can be used during the hiring process to provide deeper insights into candidates' personality and behavioral tendencies. I am a proponent of such testing, especially for leadership roles. These tests, however, are only a part of the process and cannot guarantee an alignment of values.

The higher up a person is in the organization, the more critical it becomes to ensure alignment of values. Despite the best intentions, testing, and interviewing, sometimes people still come into the organization with mismatched values.

In such cases, leaders must rise to the occasion and address emerging issues as soon as they become apparent. Others in the organization see the mismatch, and in fact often see it before the leader does. Those team members are watching closely to see if, when, and how the matters are addressed.

Our Values

The values of my organization are as follows:

- **Integrity**

- **Excellence**

- **Stewardship**

- **Compassion**

- **Accountability**

Of course, I am biased, but I think these are a pretty solid set of values. In fact, you may find these same values touted by many other companies. For example, integrity, excellence, and accountability could be applicable to any financial-services-related entity. Compassion and stewardship might be included in the values of many faith-based organizations.

But two people with the same personality traits will live them out in very different ways. Likewise, different companies will embody the same values in different ways.

For faith-based organizations, values are properly understood in light of the beliefs of the sponsoring entity.

Because Concordia Plan Services is a Lutheran Christian organization, our values reflect who we are in Christ. We live out our values as part of our sanctified lives. Our values permeate our work as we serve in the vocations God has called us to.

The book of James tells us that "faith apart from works is dead" (James 2:26). Our faith forms, shapes, and defines our values. In turn, our values form, shape, and define how we work and how we serve.

Integrity, excellence, stewardship, compassion, and accountability are properly understood for our organization when considered with a biblical worldview as seen through a Lutheran Christian lens.

FAITH SHAPES VALUES.

VALUES DRIVE BEHAVIORS.

This type of foundation is essential for anyone desiring to lead by faith. Faith shapes values. Values drive behaviors.

Organizational Values in Action

While they are present in regular conversations and the course of everyday events, values are tested and best demonstrated during challenging times or when tough decisions need to be made.

Values in and of themselves do not tell you which decision to make. But they can tell you *how* decisions must be made.

For our organization, the values sometimes seem to conflict with one another. For example, compassion might suggest that we grant exceptions liberally. However, we administer qualified employee benefit plans that are governed by legal documents. Integrity, stewardship, and accountability would compel us to hold the line on exceptions.

Here is a clear example of why values cannot tell you what decision should be made. Our values could lead us to accept or reject any appeal from those we serve. For example, we could move to quickly deny a request and point to the value of stewardship. And we would feel justified that our decision was supported by our values. The decision might be correct according to one value, but it still may not be right.

Instead of looking at how the values conflict with one another, we need to consider how our values complement and work with one another.

Ephesians 4:15 calls us to speak the truth in love. Even if an answer must be no, that answer can be delivered with love and compassion. With integrity, we can look into the facts and circumstances of the situation and consider whether an exception is warranted. With compassion, we consider the position of our plan member. There are times when a scenario was not considered when the language of the plan was drafted. In this case, the values work together to bring forward an amendment to the plan for our board of directors to approve.

> WE NEED TO CONSIDER HOW OUR VALUES COMPLEMENT AND WORK WITH ONE ANOTHER.

In other cases, we bring forward alternative solutions or options for the member. Perhaps we cannot approve the appeal, but we can bring forward a new alternative for addressing the underlying issue.

When this is working well, the values are not in conflict. Rather, they work together and complement one another as we determine the best path forward for fulfilling our mission while upholding each of our values.

Another great example came during the global COVID pandemic. Our organization knew that our customers needed us to continue to serve them during these challenging and unprecedented times. Our ministries and members themselves were struggling to serve during the pandemic. Schools and churches looked for creative solutions to continue their respective missions in the midst of chaos.

The organization was accountable to deliver results. Yet we had no structure for remote work.

Our values compelled us to proactive action. The first phase involved getting people set up in their homes with computers and workstations. Calls were routed to cell phones. Over time, our values of integrity, excellence, and stewardship moved us to improve processes and remove the bottlenecks created by the rush to remote work.

Through all of this, we needed another value of ours: compassion—not only for those we serve, but also for our colleagues.

We were thrown into a new working world with no idea of the rules or norms. Parents had to deal with their children now learning from home over video. Spouses and loved ones lost jobs. Households were devastated. Some employees contracted the virus, and their health was severely impacted. We heard stories of coworkers or loved ones in the ICU.

Galatians 6:2 continued to run through my head during that time: "Bear one another's burdens, and so fulfill the law of Christ." For our organization, it was a time to lead with grace. Yes, we needed to continue to get the work done; our values and our mission were very clear. But the circumstances also called for compassion and understanding.

> **IT WAS A TIME TO LEAD WITH GRACE.**

We all recall the amount of misinformation thrown around at that time. Very few people knew what to think or believe. Fear ruled those days, months, and even years now with an angry fist. Compassion, grace, and understanding were mighty and effective antidotes to that fear.

Our decisions and actions during the pandemic were not perfect. But in the end, our team did an incredible job of navigating those storms. Our employee satisfaction and engagement actually increased during the pandemic. I attribute this to the fact that we were guided by our values as we strove to fulfill our mission.

A Leader's Values

Values, along with missions and visions, are incredibly important for an organization. Well-articulated and executed missions, visions, and values can propel an entity forward in powerful ways.

Leaders also need to have their own set of values.

Like organizational values, the values of leaders do not prescribe certain actions to be taken. Leadership values are not a template for decision-making but, rather, a framework through which to deliberate and evaluate each decision.

Leaders' values are deeply personal. Not personal in a sense that they are to be private or only internalized—rather, they are deeply personal because they were given by the all-knowing and all-powerful Creator! He has created and appointed each of us to serve in our respective roles, and He has uniquely gifted each one of us for service. That includes the values that make up our moral fabric.

Values are also personal because they play out uniquely in every leader's life and journey.

Just as an organization's culture is largely determined by its values, leaders have their own leadership style that is highly influenced by their values. I will take it even one step further: if one's leadership style is not connected with one's values, issues of authenticity and credibility will inevitably arise. This is especially true for Christian leaders.

Our faith should play a critical role in shaping our leadership style. But that does not mean that Christian leaders all have the same leadership style. Just as God has created and gifted us differently, so our leadership styles are different. But the leadership style and behaviors of Christian leaders should be aligned and congruent with their faith. If they are not, then we will lose authenticity and credibility.

> IF ONE'S LEADERSHIP STYLE IS NOT CONNECTED WITH ONE'S VALUES, ISSUES OF AUTHENTICITY AND CREDIBILITY WILL INEVITABLY ARISE.

Thanks be to God that He does not call us to be perfect. But He does call us to be faithful!

When our decisions, actions, or behaviors fail to align with our values as Christian leaders, there is hope and forgiveness at the foot of the cross! We are forgiven and restored so that we can continue to lead in the roles that He has called us to serve in.

My Values

A number of years ago, I participated in an exercise to help me discover my values. Now, many years later, those values still hold true. Although I may not think about them on a daily basis, I can see how they have worked together to mold and shape me as a leader and in all other aspects of my life.

As I HAVE MATURED AS A LEADER, MY VALUES HAVE MATURED ALONG WITH ME.

I would not define these values the same way today as I did back when the list was created. Nor do they play out the same way today as they did back then. I am older, more experienced, and hopefully wiser today than I was back then. As I have matured as a leader, my values have matured along with me.

These are my values:

- **FAITH:** All that I am begins with One who created and redeemed me, a lost and condemned sinner. He has given me life now and into eternity. He has gifted me to serve in each of the vocations He has called me to.

- **FAMILY:** The greatest joys in life come in being a husband to my wife, a father to my sons and daughters-in-law, and a grandpa to my grandchildren. They also come in being a son, a brother, and a brother-in-law. God has richly blessed me with an incredible and loving family!

- **INTEGRITY:** It is my hope and prayer that I am a man of integrity. Integrity encompasses attributes such as honesty, trustworthiness, and principled thought and action. It involves self-discipline and consistency. Integrity means that one has the moral courage to do the right thing. In my opinion, integrity is required of every leader.

- **EXCELLENCE:** Perfection is impossible. And at the other end of the spectrum, we can be tempted to do just enough to get by. But I believe that God has created us and calls us to pursue excellence as we live out our vocations (see Philippians 4:8). As a coach on the field and as a leader of a company, I challenge myself and my teams to excellence in all that we do. Excellence calls us to be better to-day than we were yesterday—to learn and to grow from our experiences.

- **MEANINGFUL WORK:** There was a time in my life that I was just working at a job. The feeling was shallow and incomplete. Perhaps that is why this value resonated with me after I came to work for my organization. We take care of church work-ers. We improve their lives and the lives of their families, helping them be well so they can serve well. And we save millions of dollars for our min-istries in the process! Those dollars stay at the local ministry, enabling and supporting ministry in that place.

- **HEALTH:** I have always been involved in sports and other activities, and I enjoy the fact that I can still be active after age 60! Exercise provides not only physical benefits but mental benefits as well. I love running (okay, not so much the actual running part) and biking in the quiet of the mornings. It is a time to refresh my mind and process things. It is a time of prayer and reflection. On days when I ex-ercise in the morning, I feel better and more alert. I feel a resilience of youth! I know that others are watching me as a leader, so it is important for me to model the behaviors that I encourage in others.

Your Values

Have you identified the values of your organization? How about your personal values as a leader or an emerging leader?

I have no magic formula or template to follow. There are tools and resources available, and there are consultants who can assist you with the process.

But I do know this: those values must be discovered. Both in your organization and for you personally, the values are already there.

For your organization, they are embedded in your culture. They are what your people have already determined them to be. Can they be changed? Yes, it is possible to change the culture of an organization, but that process is long and challenging. It will require perseverance and all of your leadership abilities.

What about individual values—can they be changed? God can and does change hearts and minds, and with those changes, our values can be changed as well. However, I do not believe that, on our own, we can change our values. They are part of who we are. They may grow and mature as we grow and mature as leaders. But God created each of us to be unique—He made you to be you. Embrace your values as part of the leader God has created you to be!

EMBRACE YOUR VALUES AS PART OF THE LEADER GOD HAS CREATED YOU TO BE!

Leadership journeys are personal. Your journey is yours and yours alone. God has created and equipped you for service. And the values He instilled in you are part of His preparing you for His service!

LEADING
by FAITH

· · · · · · · · · · · · · · · · · ·

Writing a book has been a journey for me—or perhaps I should call it an interesting turn in my leadership journey. I want to thank you for coming along with me as we traversed this winding road together.

One of my hobbies is photography, and I enjoy having my camera with me whenever my wife and I are out hiking. There is one particular type of picture I like to take while out on hikes, and I have many versions from various locations—the trail ahead disappearing into the trees. You cannot see what lies ahead, but the trail beckons you forward.

Leadership is like that. You are ever moving forward but never certain of what waits around the bend. The trees often obscure the view ahead.

> **YOU CANNOT SEE WHAT LIES AHEAD, BUT THE TRAIL BECKONS YOU FORWARD.**

Like any analogy, this imagery has its limitations. If we put too much emphasis on the image of a trail disappearing into the forest ahead, we might imagine our journeys are isolated and independent. And at times, that sense of being alone is very real.

But in reality, our leadership journeys intertwine with others who are also walking their paths. Our journey is ours alone, but along the way, it interacts and interweaves with other people's journeys. Their journey may have an impact on ours. Likewise, our journey may impact others.

Perhaps a different analogy is more appropriate.

A Lesson from Normandy

Several years ago, my wife and I had the opportunity to tour Normandy. It ended up being a private tour as no one else signed up for the group tour that day! Walking the beaches, the villages, and the cemetery made for one of the most profound and moving days of my life.

That day in Normandy, I realized that I had been approaching history all wrong.

I used to think about history in terms of the big story. I recall having to memorize years, kings and other rulers, nations and wars, and other macro events. Some of it caught my interest, but rote memorization was never my thing. That approach to history was not compelling for me.

Walking through Normandy, I finally understood that history is not about the macro events. History is made up of millions upon millions of small stories. And these individual stories intertwine with countless other individual stories to weave a tapestry.

Each soldier was a thread. The tapestry of Normandy comprises each individual thread woven together to create the whole. Some threads played a role throughout the entire tapestry. Some threads were cut short. But each played a part in the story of D-Day.

> INDIVIDUAL STORIES INTERTWINE WITH COUNTLESS OTHER INDIVIDUAL STORIES TO WEAVE A TAPESTRY.

Our guide, Colin, told us stories at each location on our tour—stories of individual people. Individuals who made decisions. Individuals who took action. Individuals who made mistakes. Individuals who showed tremendous bravery. Individuals who simply did what needed to be done. Colin challenged us to look at our surroundings through the eyes of those individuals. He encouraged us to see and understand the events as they played out for that soldier, at that time, in that place.

This image became real to me as we stood inside a church that had changed hands several times during those first days of the invasion. Each exchange came with new stories as first the Americans and then the Germans captured and recaptured the town and the church. The walls and floors still bore the scars of war.

The story of Normandy is not about the generals or the Atlantic Wall, although they are also part of the tapestry. The success of the Allies came down to the will and spirit of the American soldier, individually and collectively.

Something Much Bigger than Me

A tapestry is so much more than the individual threads that it is composed of. No one thread is more important than another. Each thread, by itself, is highly dispensable. It is only the interwoven collection of threads that makes the tapestry and the picture complete.

As a leader, I am only one thread in the tapestry of God's church. He can do just fine without me in the mix. And yet, He chose to weave me into the work of His church.

This tapestry also flows through time. My thread has a beginning and an end, but it interweaves with those who served before me, through decades of service and then on to those who will follow.

God has called and equipped you to be part of the same tapestry. Our placement and our roles within the tapestry are different. And our pathways, our leadership journeys, are different. And yet our journeys are interwoven into the larger fabric and picture.

Understanding my place as a leader in the larger tapestry of God's kingdom gives me great hope and encouragement. It provides confidence and comfort. It provides strength and a resilience.

Alternatives to Leading by Faith

Through this entire book, I have encouraged you to lead by faith. Before we come to a close, let's consider the alternatives.

If not by faith, then how would one lead?

Two alternatives exist: leading by fear or leading by fact.

> IF NOT BY FAITH, THEN HOW WOULD ONE LEAD?

Leaders choose fear when they look outside themselves with trepidation. Lacking any source of strength or confidence, they then turn back inside themselves.

Fear can be a very powerful motivator, but it ultimately brings destruction.

On the beaches of Normandy, fear led soldiers to seek safety by staying on the beach. After surviving the trip to the beach from the landing vessel, through the waves and barrage of bullets, they took sanctuary behind whatever debris could be found. But safety was only an illusion as long as the Germans held the higher ground. Fear implored soldiers to stay put. But fear was telling them a lie.

Fear leads to paralysis. Fear also clouds our judgment, keeping us from making good decisions. Inaction, or desperate action, ensues.

Fear can also cause a leader to lash out, like a cornered animal. Again, with clouded judgement and a lack of clarity, fear can bring behaviors that are destructive to the team and to others.

Proverbs 29:25 tells us this about fear: "The fear of man lays a snare, but whoever trusts in the LORD is safe."

Fear has no role to play for Christian leaders. Faith is too powerful.

> FEAR HAS NO ROLE TO PLAY FOR CHRISTIAN LEADERS. FAITH IS TOO POWERFUL.

The second alternative to leading by faith is to lead by facts. The problems associated with leading with fear are fairly evident. The problems that come with leading by fact are far more insidious.

Now please do not get me wrong—of course leaders must seek out and carefully weigh the facts when making decisions. We are to use the brains God has given us! We understand that God has given us the ability to think and to reason. Even our intelligence is a gift from Him to be used for His purpose and to His glory.

But leading by fact instead of faith means that we are relying most on our own understanding, on our own intellect. Such leaders may end up putting themselves in the place of God or even denying Him altogether.

Proverbs 14:12 tells us: "There is a way that seems right to a man, but its end is the way to death." This is a warning against relying on your own knowledge and understanding of the facts and circumstances.

Instead, consider this encouragement from Proverbs 3:5–6:

> **Trust in the LORD with all your heart, and do not lean on your own understanding. In all your ways acknowledge Him, and He will make straight your paths.**

A similar encouragement is found in Proverbs 16:3:

> **Commit your work to the LORD, and your plans will be established.**

Facts look inward for answers and solutions and directions, whereas faith calls us to look upward to God, who has created and called us!

Leading by Faith

There is a role within an athletic team that only certain players can fulfill. In the college ranks, it is typically a senior (which today means a fourth-, fifth-, or sixth-year player). In the pros, it is the seasoned veteran. This position is critical for the success of the team and for the growth and development of younger players. The role is informal rather than formal. And I find myself more and more in this situation.

I am referring to the leaders in the locker room: those experienced players who have quite a few games under their belts and hopefully still have a few more seasons in them. Their careers have seen ups and downs, successes and failures. They have overcome injuries and other hardships.

These players have come to a point in their careers when they know and embrace a new set of responsibilities. They have the honor and privilege of encouraging the next generation of players.

Today, I see that I am in that role more and more. It is a duty I accept with humility and respect for those who did the same for me.

This book is primarily for leaders and emerging leaders within the church that I have loved and served for over twenty-five years. It is also intended for those who serve in different places and in different ways.

Perhaps any reader can find something good and useful in these pages, but I believe that the greatest value will be for those who know Christ as Lord and Savior.

Leading by faith is so much more than a book title or philosophy. It is an aspirational statement for Christian leaders because leading by faith drives out fear and despair!

We can lead by faith because of the certain hope we have within us—not because of anything we have done, but because of what Christ has done for us through His death and resurrection.

> WE CAN LEAD BY FAITH BECAUSE OF THE CERTAIN HOPE WE HAVE WITHIN US.

If we truly believe that God has called and equipped us to be leaders in this time and in this place, then we can serve boldly and with conviction!

I do not know where God is taking me on the remainder of my leadership journey. I do not even know what lies around the next turn. But I do know that He holds everything in His mighty hands. By His grace and by His power, I can lead by faith, not by sight.

And He will do the same for you.

To God alone be the glory!

Acknowledgments

I want to begin by giving all thanks and honor to my Lord and Savior, Jesus Christ. All that I have and have done has come through His grace and provision.

His greatest gift to me is my wife, Janell. None of what I have done would have been possible without her constant love and support. As my duties often took me away from home, she faithfully managed our household and cared for our three sons—often on her own! Today she gives the same love and care to our wonderful grandchildren. Janell, thank you for all that you have done to love and support me through this journey. I could not have done it without you.

This book has become a family project of sorts. Thank you to my sons and daughters-in-law for your support and encouragement. A special thanks to Maddie for your creative work on my logo.

Thanks to the Concordia Plan Services board, who gave me the opportunity to lead this incredible organization that cares for the workers of our church! It has been a real honor to serve in this unique role.

I want to thank the team at Concordia Publishing House, and especially my editor, Jamie. The original draft that landed on her desk put her editorial skills to the test! All that is good is a result of her work; the rest can be blamed on me.

Thank you to my readers for coming with me on this journey. My hope and prayer is that this book will be a blessing and an encouragement to you.

To God alone be the glory!

About the Author

J im Sanft is a seasoned nonprofit executive, having served as president and CEO of Concordia Plan Services for more than fifteen years. This follows ten years of service in executive leadership roles at CPS and just over ten years working as an actuary in the group insurance industry.

During his tenure as CEO, Jim has developed expertise in three key areas of executive leadership:

1. **Leading through times of crisis**

2. **Building coalitions**

3. **Growing a high-performing culture**

Concordia Plan Services manages the employee benefit programs of The Lutheran Church—Missouri Synod, including retirement, health, life, and disability plans. Operating much like a small insurance company, this entity of the church has a mission to serve ministries and to care for church workers so that the Word of God may spread! CPS has around five billion dollars of assets under management and serves thirty thousand church workers, plus dependents and retirees.

During his tenure as CEO, Jim has guided his organization through challenging times, including the Global Financial Crisis, the Affordable Care Act, and the global COVID-19 pandemic. All three presented significant challenges to the CPS business model and challenged CPS's ability to fulfill its mission.

Jim is an active leader in the broader church benefit community and actively partners with his counterparts in other denominational benefits organizations. He has served on the board of directors of the Church Benefits Association and currently serves as chair of the Church Alliance. The Church Alliance actively works with legislators and regulators in Washington,

DC, to educate and inform them of the unique role that church plans play in support of their respective denominations. As chair, Jim frequently meets with senators, members of congress, and their staff to advocate for church plans. During his time as chair, the Church Alliance has successfully moved issues through the legislative pipeline and into key bills that were passed into law.

During his time at Concordia Plan Services, Jim has recruited and developed a high-performing team. The CPS team has been recognized multiple times as a top workplace in St. Louis and has been named as a top workplace nationally. Jim has cultivated a strong organizational culture built on a foundation of strong values.

Jim was awarded a doctor of law *honoris causa* by his alma mater, Concordia University, Nebraska, where he earned a bachelor of science in education. He has also earned a master of science in mathematics and statistics from the University of Nebraska, Lincoln.

Prior to serving the church, Jim worked within the group insurance and employee benefit industry. He is a Fellow of the Society of Actuaries and a Member of the American Academy of Actuaries. In total, he has more than thirty-five years of experience in insurance and employee benefits.

Jim is married to the love of his life, Janell, and they make their home in Columbia, Illinois. They have three sons, three daughters-in-laws, and the cutest set of grandchildren ever!

Jim and Janell enjoy traveling together and hiking in the splendor of God's creation. They feel especially blessed to spend time with their family—especially their grandchildren!